外国人対応に
役立つ

和英対照

税務ハンドブック

税制解説の英訳 & 税務用語辞典

FAIR CONSULTING GROUP
税理士法人フェアコンサルティング編

Commentary
and
dictionary
on
JAPANESE
tax system
and
terms

税務経理協会

はじめに

本書は、日本人以外の納税者に英語で日本の税制を説明する必要がある実務家の方のために作成いたしました。コロナ禍の最中でも、日本で新たに事業展開を始める企業や来日外国人は少なくありません。日本は今も魅力的な投資対象として海外から映っているのだと感じます。しかし、日本の税制度は複雑であり、諸外国にない日本独自ともいえるようなルールも存在することから、日本で事業を行うためには、日本の税制度に対する理解は避けて通ることができません。それにもかかわらず、日本に進出する企業や来日して働く外国人の方にわかりやすく日本の税制度を説明することを支援する書籍はこれまでほとんど見られなかったように感じます。これが本書執筆の動機でした。

日本の税制を海外の人たちに説明する際に気を付けなければならないのは、単に日本語の専門用語を英語に直訳した単語を示しても、こちらが思うように理解してはもらえないということです。大切なことは、その単語の意味するところをしっかりと説明することです。その上で、その説明する概念を表す語として、本書に示す訳語を提示していただければ、日本の税制に不慣れな方にもしっかりと理解をしてもらえるものと信じています。

本書は、企画のお話をいただいてから日の目を見るまでに随分長い期間を要してしまいました。その間、決して諦めることなく支えてくださった税務経理協会の中村謙一氏の粘り強さに深く敬意を表して、ここに感謝を捧げたいと思います。本書が、異なる文化背景を持つ納税者とのコミュニケーションに格闘される実務家の助けになれば、これに勝る喜びはありません。

2022 年 12 月

税理士法人フェアコンサルティング

本書の使い方

本書は以下の３部構成となっています。

①【和英対照】税制解説の英訳

外資系内国法人、外国法人日本支店、居住者又は非居住者となる外国人が日頃直面しやすい日本の主要な租税法上の論点の概要を、和英対訳の形で解説したものです。外国人クライアントに英語で日本の税制について説明する必要がある場合に、英語表現の参考となれば幸いです。なお、各項目はわかりやすさを優先して省略した事項もありますので、個別の事項に関しては必ずそれぞれの該当する税法の規定を確認し、適宜説明するようにしてください。

なお、本解説は、国税庁英語版ホームページに掲載されている各種解説（法人税の基本的な計算方法、所得税の基本的な計算方法、消費税の基本的な計算方法、リバースチャージ方式の解説等）と重複する部分は割愛し、国税庁からあまり情報発信されていない事項を中心に構成していますので、ご承知おきください。

②【税務辞典】和英編

○　日本の税制度に関わる用語を中心に、税務から切り離すことのできない会計や法律等に関する用語も一部掲載しました。

○　用語については、OECDで使用されている英国式のスペリングを採用していますのでご注意ください。

○　単なる単語だけでなく、句の形でなければ意味をなさない用語（例：不服申立てをする）については、可能な限り句の形で掲載するようにしました。

○　日本の税制度に関わる用語には、定まった訳語が存在しないものも多くあります。そのようなものについては、適宜日本の税制度を知らない外国人がその内容を理解できるような訳語を付すようにしました。

○　日本語見出しにおける頭字語（アクロニム）については、それを用いることが日本語の文脈でも自然とされるケースに使用しています（例：代理人PE）。

○　解説が必要と考えられる用語については、適宜 **解説** としてその意義を簡潔に示しました。

○　使い方を明示した方が読者の便宜に資すると思われる場合に、適宜 **例** としてその用語の使用例を示しました。

○　使用法に注意を要する語には、適宜 **注** として注意すべき点を示しました。

○　用語中の（　）は、その（　）内の語が省略可能であることを示しています。

○　訳語中の（　）は、直前の訳語の補足情報を記載しています。

○　用語中の［　］は、その［　］内の語をその直前の語に置き換えることができることを示しています。

③　【税務辞典】英和編

○　外国人と英語でコミュニケーションをとるに際し必要と考えられる税制度に関わる用語を中心に、税務から切り離すことのできない会計や法律等に関する用語も一部掲載しました。

○　用語については、OECDで使用されている英国式のスペリングを採用していますのでご注意ください。

○　単なる単語だけでなく、句の形で一まとまりの意味をなす用語については、可能な限り句の形で掲載するようにしました。

○　頭字語（アクロニム）の見出しついては、その語の本来の表記を示すのみにとどめ、その本来の表記の見出しにおいて（　）の中にその頭字語を示すとともに、訳語及び解説等を示しています。

○　訳語は、税務・会計で用いられるものに限って掲載しています。

○　解説が必要と考えられる用語については、適宜 **解説** としてその意義を簡潔に示しました。

○　使い方を明示した方が読者の便宜に資すると思われる場合に、適宜 **例** としてその用語の使用例を示しました。

○　使用法に注意を要する語には、適宜 **注** として注意すべき点を示しました。

○　米国独自の用語については 米 として示しました。

○　用語中の（　）は、その（　）内の語が省略可能であることを示しています。

○　訳語中の（　）は、直前の訳語の補足情報を記載しています。

○　用語中の［　］は、その［　］内の語をその直前の語に置き換えることができることを示しています。

CONTENTS

【和英対照】
税制解説の英訳

1 租税制度

1 国税と地方税

日本には、課税主体が国である国税と、地方自治体である地方税の２種類の税があります。所得を課税標準とする国税としては所得税及び法人税があります。そして、所得税若しくは法人税の課税標準又は税額をその課税標準とする地方税として、住民税及び事業税があります。また、代表的な間接税である消費税は、国税部分と地方税部分からなります。その他、国税には相続税、印紙税等、地方税には固定資産税、事業所税、自動車税、不動産取得税等多様な税が存在します。

なお、個人の場合、2011 年に発生した東日本大震災からの復興に係る財源を広く調達する目的で、2037 年までの間、その納付する所得税の他に、納付する所得税に 2.1 %を乗じて求められる復興特別所得税を納付する必要があります。源泉徴収される所得税についても、復興特別所得税が併せて徴収されます。

2 課税の方式（申告納税方式、賦課課税方式と源泉徴収方式）

(1) 課税方式の種類

日本では、納付すべき税額の確定方法は以下の３種類があります。

	方式	内容
1	申告納税方式	納税者の申告によって納付すべき税額が確定する方式
2	賦課課税方式	納付すべき税額が行政組織からの処分（通知）によって確定する方式

1 TAXATION SYSTEM

1 National tax and local tax

In Japan, there are 2 types of taxes, national tax, of which the sovereign of taxation is the country, and local tax, of which the sovereign of taxation is the local government. National taxes for which income is the taxable basis are income tax and corporate tax. Local taxes for which the taxable basis of income tax or corporate tax or the tax amount is the taxable basis are inhabitant tax and business tax. Consumption tax, which is a typical indirect tax, consists of the national tax portion and the local tax portion. In addition, there are various taxes such as inheritance tax and stamp duty in national taxes and fixed asset tax, business office tax, automobile tax and real estate acquisition tax in local taxes. Individuals are required to pay, until 2037, in addition to the income tax, a restoration special income tax, which is calculated by multiplying the income tax by 2.1%, for the purpose of broadly raising funds for reconstruction from the Great East Japan Earthquake that occurred in 2011. For income taxes withheld at source, restoration special income tax will be levied at the same time.

2 Taxation system (Self-assessment system, official assessment system and withholding tax system)

(1) Types of taxation systems

In Japan, there are three methods to determine tax liability.

	System	Details
1	Self-assessment system	Method in which tax liability is determined by the taxpayer's self-assessment
2	Official assessment system	Method in which tax liability is determined by a disposition (notification) from an administrative organization

3	源泉徴収方式	納付すべき税額が、納税義務の成立と同時に特別な手続きを要することなく確定する方式

(2) 納税義務の成立と確定

納税義務は、それぞれの租税の種類に応じて、原則として以下のように定められています。

租税の種類	納税義務の成立の時
法人税	事業年度終了の時
所得税（申告所得税）	その年 12 月 31 日の終了の時
所得税（源泉所得税）	源泉徴収の要件が満たされた時
相続税	相続、遺贈等による財産の取得の時
消費税	課税資産の譲渡等又は特定課税仕入れをした時
住民税	（個人）その年 1 月 1 日現在住所を有していること （法人）その地方自治体の区域内に事務所又は事業所を有すること
事業税	（個人・法人共通）その地方自治体の区域内に事務所又は事業所を有すること

また、それぞれの租税の納税義務は、その納付すべき税額の確定の方式に応じ、次の時期に確定します。

方式	納税義務の確定の時期
申告納税方式	納税者が納税申告書を税務署等に提出した時
賦課課税方式	行政官庁による賦課決定処分の時
源泉徴収方式	源泉徴収の要件が満たされた時

(3) 法定納期限

法定納期限とは、国税に関する法律の規定により国税を納付すべき期限をいい、原則として法定されている申告期限（法定申告期限）と同じ日となります。

3	Withholding tax system	Method in which tax liability is determined without any special procedures at the same time as the establishment of the tax obligation

(2) Establishment and determination of tax obligation

The tax obligation is stipulated as follows, in principle, according to the type of tax.

Type of tax	Time of establishment of tax obligation
Corporate tax	At the end of the business year
Income tax (Self-assessed income tax)	At the end of December 31 of that year
Income tax (Withholding income tax)	When the withholding requirement is satisfied
Inheritance tax	When property is acquired by inheritance, devise, etc.
Consumption tax	When a taxable asset is transferred, or a specific taxable purchase is made
Inhabitant tax	(Individual) Having an address as of January 1 of that year (Corporation) Having offices or business establishments in the area of a local government
Business tax	(Individual/Corporation) Having offices or business establishments in the area of a local government

In addition, the tax obligation for each tax is determined at the following time according to the method of determining the tax liability.

System	Time of determination of tax obligation
Self-assessment system	When the taxpayer submits the tax return to the tax office, etc.
Official assessment system	When the administrative agency determines the tax liability
Withholding tax system	When the withholding requirement is satisfied

(3) Statutory due date for tax payment

The statutory due date for tax payment refers to the due date for the payment of national taxes pursuant to the provisions of laws concerning national taxes. In principle, the date is the same as the statutory due date for filing tax returns.

3 附帯税（ペナルティ）

(1) 附帯税の種類

国税に関する申告書の提出や納税を定められた期限までにしなかった場合や、事実を偽って申告書を提出したりした場合には、それぞれの行為に対応する附帯税である延滞税又は加算税が、本来の税額に加えて課されます。

附帯税が課される行為・状態	課される附帯税
納付すべき税額を定められた期限までに完納しない場合	延滞税
修正申告書の提出により、その修正申告書の提出の直前に提出された確定申告書又は修正申告書に記載した納付すべき税額が不足することとなった場合	過少申告加算税
期限後申告の場合又は期限後申告に係る修正申告書を提出した場合	無申告加算税
源泉徴収による国税がその納期限までに完納されなかった場合	不納付加算税
納期限を延長している場合	利子税
納付すべき税額の計算の基礎となる事実を仮装又は隠蔽し、その仮装又は隠蔽したところに基づき納税申告書を提出した場合	重加算税

（注 1）更正処分による場合は省略しています。

なお、地方税にも上記と同様のペナルティである延滞金又は加算金があります。

上記の各種ペナルティは、利子税を除き、所得税又は法人税の所得計算上必要経費又は損金の額に算入されません。

3 Accessory tax (Penalty)

(1) Type of accessory tax

In the event that a taxpayer fails to file a tax return or pay taxes related to national taxes by the stipulated due date, or submits a tax return by falsifying facts, delinquency tax or additional tax, corresponding to the respective act, will be imposed in addition to the original tax amount.

Acts or conditions for which accessory tax is imposed	Accessory tax
When tax liability is not paid in full by the stipulated due date	Delinquency tax
Where the filing of an amended tax return results in a shortfall in the tax liability as stated in the final tax return or amended tax return filed immediately prior to the filing of the amended tax return	Additional tax on underreport
Where a tax return is filed after the due date or an amended tax return pertaining to late filing is filed	Late filing tax
When national tax withheld at source is not paid in full by the due date	Additional tax on nonpayment of withholding tax
When tax payment due date is extended	Interest tax
Where a taxpayer has disguised or concealed the facts that form the basis for the calculation of the tax liability and submitted a tax return based on such disguise or concealment.	Heavy additional tax

(Note 1) Cases due to tax reassessment are omitted.

Local taxes are also subject to the same penalties as above, i.e., delinquent charge or additional charge.

The above accessory taxes, excluding interest tax, are not included in necessary expenses or deductible expenses for income tax or corporate tax purposes.

(2) 附帯税の税率

附帯税	原則的な税率
延滞税	次の(1)と(2)の合計額 (1) 納期限までの期間及び納期限の翌日から2月を経過する日までの期間 年「7.3％」と延滞税特例基準割合（平均貸付割合(注)＋1％）のいずれか低い割合 (2) 納期限の翌日から2月を経過する日の翌日以後 年「14.6％」と「延滞税特例基準割合＋7.3％」のいずれか低い割合 (注) 平均貸付割合とは、各年の前年の11月30日までに財務大臣が告示する割合をいいます。
過少申告加算税	次の(1)と(2)の合計額 (1) 追加納付額の5％（税務調査が行われ、更正又は決定処分がされることを予知して修正申告書を提出した場合は10％） (2) (1)の追加納付額のうち、直前までに提出した申告書によって納付すべき税額の合計額と50万円とのいずれか多い金額を超える部分の金額の5％
無申告加算税	次の(1)から(3)までの合計額 (1) 納付税額の15％(税務調査が行われ、更正又は決定処分がされることを予知して提出された期限後申告書でない場合は10％、更正又は決定がされることを予知しておらず、かつ、その申告に係る国税の調査通知前に提出された期限後申告書については、5％) (2) 期限後申告又は期限後申告後に提出した修正申告書によって納付すべき税額の合計額が50万円を超える場合のその超える部分の金額の5％ (3) 期限後申告書又はその期限後申告書に係る修正申告書の提出の日の前日から5年前の日までの間にこれらの申告書に係る税目に付き無申告加算税又は重加算税を課された場合には、(1)の納付税額の10％
不納付加算税	期限後に納付された源泉所得税額の10％
利子税	年「7.3％」と利子税特例基準割合（平均貸付割合(注)＋0.5％）のいずれか低い割合 (注) 延滞税の注参照

(2) Rate of accessory tax

Accessory tax	Principle tax rate
Delinquency tax	Total amount of the following (1) and (2) (1) Period up to the due date for tax payment and period up to the day on which two months have elapsed from the day following the due date for tax payment "7.3%" per annum or special standard rate for delinquency tax (average loan ratio(Note) + 1%), whichever is lower. (2) On or after the day following the day on which two months have elapsed from the day following the due date for tax payment "14.6%" per annum or "special standard rate for delinquency tax + 7.3%", whichever is lower (Note) Average loan ratio refers to the ratio announced by the Minister of Finance by November 30 of the previous year of each year.
Additional tax on underreport	Total amount of the following (1) and (2) (1) 5% of the additional payment (10% if an amended tax return is filed in anticipation of tax reassessment or determination after tax examination) (2) Out of the additional payment referred to in (1) above, 5% of the amount in excess of either the total amount of tax liability based on the tax return filed immediately prior, or JPY 500,000, whichever is larger
Late filing tax	Total amount of the following (1) through (3) (1) 15% of the amount of tax due (10% if it is not the overdue tax return which is filed in anticipation of tax reassessment or determination after tax examination, and 5% if the tax reassessment or determination is not anticipated and overdue tax return is filed prior to the notice of examination of the national tax pertaining to the tax return) (2) In the case where the total amount of tax liability based on an overdue tax return or an amended tax return filed after the overdue tax return exceeds JPY 500,000, 5% of the amount of such excess (3) 10% of the amount of tax due under (1) if, during the period from the day before the filing date of overdue tax return or amended tax return related to such overdue tax return to the day five years before, late filing tax or heavy additional tax is imposed on the tax items pertaining to such returns
Additional tax on nonpayment of withholding tax	10% of withholding income tax paid after the due date
Interest tax	"7.3%" per annum or interest tax special standard rate (average loan ratio(Note) + 0.5%), whichever is lower. (Note) See (Note) for delinquency tax

重加算税	(1) 過少申告加算税の額の計算の基礎となるべき金額の 35 %(過少申告加算税は課されません) (2) 無申告加算税の額の計算の基礎となるべき金額の 40 %(無申告加算税は課されません) (3) 不納付加算税の額の計算の基礎となるべき金額の 35 %(不納付加算税は課されません) (4) (1)から(3)の税額の計算の基礎となる事実を仮装又は隠蔽して期限後申告書若しくは修正申告書を提出した日の前日から 5 年前の日までの間にこれらの申告書に係る税目に付き無申告加算税又は重加算税を課された場合には、(1)、(2)又は(3)の附帯税の計算の基礎となる金額の 10 %が(1)、(2)又は(3)の金額に加算されます。

(注 1) 上記は原則的な取扱いであり、上記以外の場合にも附帯税が課される場合があります。

(注 2) 更正処分による場合の記載は省略しています。

Heavy additional tax	(1) 35% of the amount to be used as the basis for calculating the amount of additional tax on underreport (additional tax on underreport is not imposed) (2) 40% of the amount to be used as the basis for calculating the amount of late filing tax (late filing tax is not imposed) (3) 35% of the amount to be used as the basis for calculating the amount of additional tax on nonpayment of withholding tax (additional tax on nonpayment of withholding tax is not imposed) (4) If, during the period up to the date on which five years have elapsed from the date on which the late filing tax or heavy additional tax was imposed, an overdue tax return or an amended tax return on the same tax items as the said late filing tax or heavy additional tax is filed by disguising or concealing the facts that form the basis for the calculation of the tax amount of (1) to (3), 10% of the amount that forms the basis for the calculation of the accessory tax of (1), (2) or (3) will be added to the amount of (1), (2) or (3).

(Note 1) The above is a general treatment, and accessory tax may be imposed in cases other than the above.
(Note 2) The description in the case of tax reassessment is omitted.

2 法人税

1 確定決算原則と税務調整（過去年度の決算の誤謬修正の影響）

日本において、法人の所得税（法人税）は、会社法に定める株主総会で承認された決算の内容に基づいて計算され申告される決まりとなっています。この決まりを「確定決算原則」といいます。この確定した決算における当期純利益の金額を出発点として、法人税法上損金にすることができない会計上の費用を当期純利益に加算し、法人税法上益金の額から除外できる会計上の収益をこの当期純利益から減算することで法人税の課税所得が計算されます。これが日本の法人税の計算に関する基本的な構造です。このため、過去年分の当期純利益が増減するような過年度遡及処理を行うと、進行年度において、当初過去年分から引き継いだ税務上の繰越利益の金額との間に齟齬が生じてしまいますので、進行年度において、過年度遡及の内容を反映した調整を行う必要が生じます。また、過去年度の売上や費用の計上漏れや過大計上といった、過去年度の課税所得に影響を及ぼす誤謬修正については、会計上の修正再表示だけでは足りず、修正申告や更正の請求といった法人税法上の是正手続きも必要となることにご留意ください。

2 収益の認識

法人税法上の収益の額は、基本的には会計上の収益の額と同様であり、いわゆる販売基準に基づいて認識します。棚卸資産であれば、原則は引渡しの時に収益を認識します。なお、ここにいう引渡しの時は、具体的には、買い手の検

2 CORPORATE TAX

1 Closed accounts principles and adjustment for taxable profit (Impact of correction of prior period errors)

In Japan, income tax for a corporation (corporate tax) is calculated and filed based on the financial statements approved at the shareholders' meeting as stipulated in the Companies Act. This rule is referred to as the "closed accounts principles."

Starting from the amount of net income in the closed accounts, taxable profit for corporate tax is calculated by adding accounting expenses that are not deductible under the Corporation Tax Act to this net income and subtracting accounting income that can be excluded from gross profit under the Corporation Tax Act from this net income. This is the basic structure for calculating corporate tax in Japan. For this reason, if the retrospective adjustment of the past fiscal year is carried out in such a way that the net income for the past fiscal year increases or decreases, there will be a discrepancy between the amount of profit carried forward for tax purposes from the past fiscal year and that carried forward stated in the financial statement approved at the shareholder's meeting in the current fiscal year. Therefore, it will be necessary to make an adjustment in the current fiscal year that reflects the contents of the retrospective processing for the past fiscal year. Also, please note that in case of correction of prior period errors affecting taxable profit for past fiscal years, such as omissions or overstatements of sales and expenses for past fiscal years, restatement of accounting purposes is not sufficient. It also requires correction procedures under the Corporation Tax Act, such as filing an amended tax return or requesting a reassessment.

2 Revenue recognition

Revenue under the Corporation Tax Act is basically the same as revenue for accounting purposes and is recognized on a sales basis. In the case of inventories, revenue is rec-

収の時、売手の出荷の時や船積みの時など、その棚卸資産の種類及び性質、その販売に係る契約の内容等に応じその引渡しの日として合理的であると認められる日のうち法人が継続してその収益計上を行うこととしている日によるものとされています。また、役務提供であれば役務の提供の時、物の引渡しを要する請負であればその引渡しの時、有価証券の譲渡であれば原則は契約の成立した日（ただし継続適用を要件として有価証券の引渡しをした日）、土地や建物であれば原則は引渡しの日（ただし継続適用を要件として契約の効力発生の日）に収益を認識します。

法人がIFRS15に基づく収益認識に関する会計基準を適用している場合には、履行義務が充足された時に税務上も収益を認識することになります。

なお、契約に基づきいかなる理由があっても顧客に返還することを要しない対価については、それが何年かにわたる継続的な役務提供の対価であっても、その受領時に収益の額として認識する必要があります。

3　費用の認識（債務確定基準）

法人税法上の費用又は損失の額については、収益の場合と同様に発生主義によって認識することを原則としています。法人税法上の費用は大きく3種類に区分されています。

(1) 収益に対応する売上原価、完成工事原価等の原価の額

(2) 販売費、一般管理費その他の費用（償却費以外の費用で事業年度終了時に債務の確定しないものを除く）

(3) 当該事業年度の損失の額で資本等取引以外の取引に係るもの

(1)の売上原価は、費用収益対応の原則によってその事業年度の収益に対応する原価を認識します。(2)の販売費、一般管理費その他の費用の額については、「債務確定基準」により、その事業年度末において債務として「確定」していないものは除かれます。「債務の確定」は、以下の3つの要件により判定されます。

ognized at the time of delivery in principle. The time of delivery referred to herein shall be, more specifically, the time of inspection by the buyer or shipping or loading by the seller, among the dates deemed reasonable as the date of delivery in accordance with the type and nature of the inventory and the contents of the sales contract, etc., the date on which the corporation is to continue to recognize revenue. In addition, revenue shall be recognized at the time of provision of services in the case of provision of services, at the time of delivery in the case of a contract requiring delivery of goods, at the time of conclusion of the contract in the case of transfer of securities, in principle (or, the date of delivery of securities subject to continuous application), at the time of delivery in the case of land or building, in principle (or, the effective date of contract subject to continuous application).

If a company applies the accounting standard for revenue recognition based on IFRS15, it will also recognize revenue for tax purposes when its performance obligations are met. Consideration that is not required to be returned to the customer for any reason under the contract should be recognized as revenue when it is received, even if it is consideration for continuous provision of services over several years.

3 Recognition of expenses (Debt Determination Standard)

As a general rule, expenses or losses under the Corporation Tax Act are recognized on an accrual basis as in the case of revenue. Expenses under the Corporation Tax Act are broadly divided into three categories.

(1) Amount of cost of sales, cost of completed construction, etc. corresponding to revenue

(2) Selling, general and administrative expenses and other expenses (excluding expenses, other than depreciation expenses, for which liabilities are not fixed at the end of the fiscal year)

(3) The amount of loss for the fiscal year pertaining to transactions other than capital transactions

For the cost of sales in (1), the cost corresponding to the revenue for the fiscal year is recognized based on the principle of matching cost with revenue.

As for the amount of selling, general and administrative expenses and other expenses

① その費用に係る債務が成立していること

② その債務に基づいて具体的な給付をすべき原因となる事実が生じていること

③ その債務の額を合理的に算定することができること

①は、例えば役務提供に係る契約が有効に成立して、サービスの受領者が代金の支払い義務を負うこととなった状態を指します。②は、例えば、①の契約に係る役務提供が完了し、代金支払い義務を履行するための条件が満たされた状態を指します。③は、支払金額算定上の不確実性が概ね排除され、支払金額を合理的に算定できる状態を指します。

この「債務確定基準」によって法人税額の計算上損金から除外される費用は、各種引当金やその他の将来の費用の見積り額であり、これは、具体的な現金の支出との対応関係がない費用、ということもできます。なお、有形固定資産や無形固定資産の減価償却費、繰延資産の償却費は、引当金などと同様現実の支出がない費用ですが、損金の額とすることができます。これは、各種資産の取得に当たり現実にされた支出の金額を時の経過に応じて費用化するという償却費の性質に鑑み、法人税法に定められている方法に従って各事業年度において一定の金額を損金の額に算入できることとされているものです。

(3)は、災害や盗難といった偶発的な原因により生じた損失であり、その事実が生じた事業年度において損金の額とすることになります。資本等取引とは、法人の資本金等の額を増加又は減少させる取引及び剰余金の分配や残余財産の分配等のことを言います。

4 役員報酬の取扱い

役員の給与は、使用人の給与と異なり、これを税務上の損金の額にするためには一定の要件を満たす必要があります。損金の額に算入できる役員給与の形態には、以下の3つのものがあります。

mentioned in (2), those which are not "fixed" as liabilities at the end of the fiscal year are excluded in accordance with the "Debt Determination Standard".
"Determination of debt" is determined by the following three requirements:

① The liability pertaining to the expenses has been established.
② A fact has arisen that causes specific benefit to be paid based on the liability.
③ The amount of such liabilities can be reasonably calculated.

① refers to, for example, a situation in which a contract for the provision of services has been validly concluded and the recipient of the services has become obligated to pay the price.
② refers to, for example, a state in which the provision of services pertaining to the contract in ① has been completed and the conditions for fulfilling the payment obligations have been met.
③ refers to a state in which uncertainty in the calculation of the payment amount has been largely eliminated and the payment amount can be reasonably calculated.

Expenses that are excluded from deductible expenses in the calculation of the amount of corporate tax under this "Debt Determination Standard" are estimated amounts of allowances and other future expenses that do not correspond to specific cash expenditures. Depreciation of tangible fixed assets and amortization of intangible fixed assets and deferred assets can be considered deductible expenses, even though, like allowances, there is no actual expenditure. Because of the nature of the depreciation expense, which is to expense the actual expenditures incurred in the acquisition of various assets over time, certain amounts may be deductible in each fiscal year in accordance with the method prescribed in the Corporation Tax Act.
(3) is a loss caused by an accidental cause such as a disaster or theft, which shall be deductible in the fiscal year in which the fact occurs. Capital transactions are transactions that increase or decrease the amount of capital, etc. of a corporation and distribution of surplus or distribution of residual property.

4 Treatment of director's compensation

The director's compensation differs from those of employees and must meet certain requirements in order to be deductible for tax purposes. There are three types of director's compensation that can be deductible.

(1)　定期同額給与

「定期同額給与」とは、役員に対する給与で、(1) 1か月以下の一定の期間ごとに支払われる（定期給与）、(2) 期中の各支給時期における支払額が同額である、という2つの要件を満たしたものをいいます。定期同額給与を改定できるのは、原則として期首から3か月以内（つまり、定時株主総会の開催時期まで）とされています。ただし、職務内容の重大な変更や経営状態が著しく悪化した場合などの臨時改定事由が生じたことによる減額改定に関しては、その改定前に支給する役員給与と改定後に支給する役員給与はそれぞれ定期同額給与として扱われることとされています。臨時改定事由以外の理由により、期首から3か月後以降に役員給与が改定されると、その改定前の給与の額と改定後の給与の額の差額は法人税法上損金不算入とされます。具体的には、以下のような損金不算入のパターンがあります。

①　ある月に賞与として通常の給与とは別に報酬を支払う場合

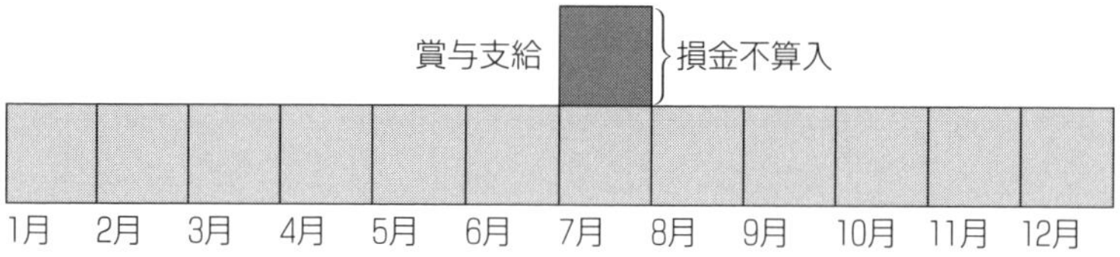

②　期首から3か月後以降に役員給与を増額する場合

その増額後と増額前の差額部分が損金不算入とされます。

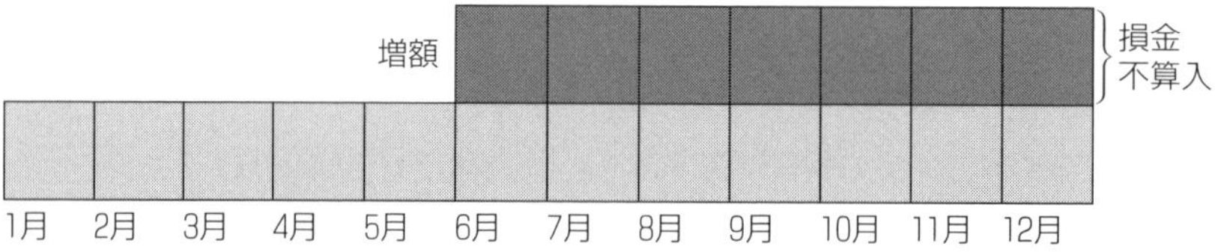

(1) Regular fixed remuneration

"Regular fixed remuneration" refers to a salary for directors that satisfies the following two requirements: (1) The salary is paid every fixed period of one month or less (regular salary) (2) The same amount is paid at each payment time during the period. In principle, regular fixed remuneration can be revised within three months from the beginning of the fiscal year (that is, up to the time of the general shareholder meeting). However, a temporary revision due to extraordinary reasons, such as a significant change in the job description or a significant deterioration in business conditions, shall be treated as a revision of regular fixed remuneration. If a director's salary is revised after three months from the beginning of the fiscal year for reasons other than temporary revisions, the difference between the previous salary and the revised salary is excluded from deductible expenses under the Corporation Tax Act. Specifically, there are the following patterns of exclusion from deductible expenses:

① In case that remuneration is paid as a bonus in a certain month in addition to ordinary salary

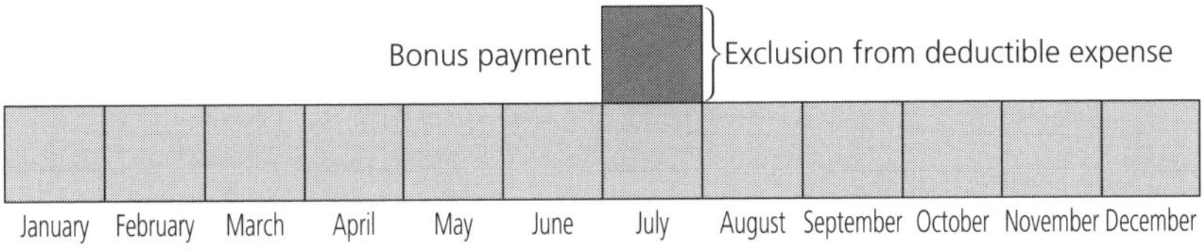

② In case that director's salary is increased after three months from the beginning of the fiscal year

The difference between the amount after the increase and the amount before the increase is excluded from deductible expense.

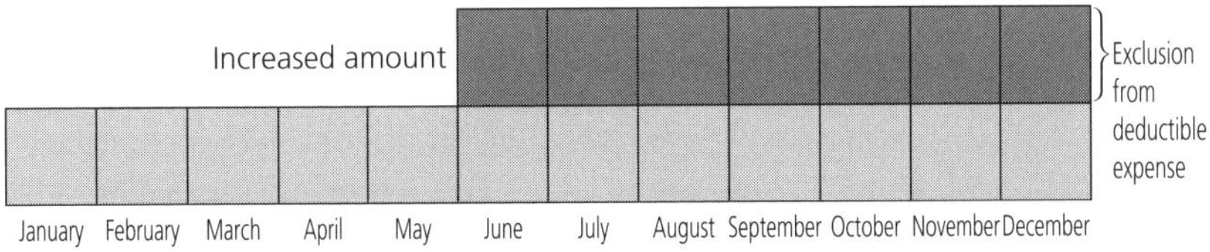

③ 期首から３か月後以降に役員給与を減額する場合

その減額前と減額後の差額部分が損金不算入とされます。

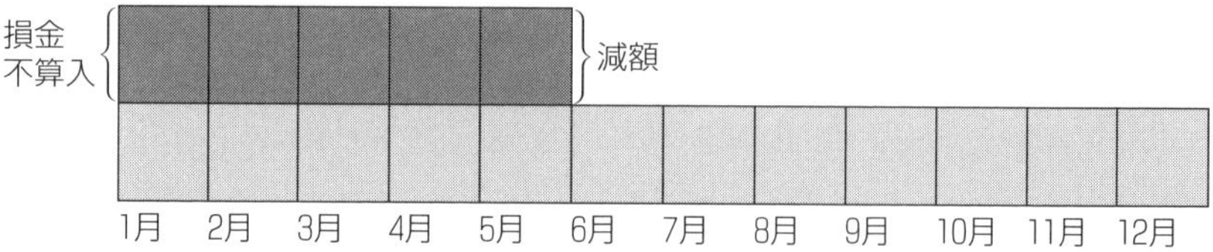

(2) 事前確定届出給与

定期同額給与、業績連動給与以外の給与で、役員に対し、所定の時期に確定額の給与を支払うことをあらかじめ税務署長に届出したものをいい、定期同額給与及び業績連動給与に該当するものは除かれます。給与としては、現金で支給されたものの他、一定の要件を満たす株式や新株予約権の交付により支給されたものについても認められます。届出の期限は、原則として、役員が職務を開始した日から１月を経過する日と期首から４月を経過する日のいずれか早い日までとされています。

(3) 業績連動給与

金銭により支給された業績連続給与及び株式又は新株予約権の交付により支給された業績連動給与のうち、それぞれ以下の要件を満たすものは、法人の所得の金額の計算上損金の額に算入することができます。

① 金銭による交付の場合

(a) 役員報酬を支給する法人が非同族会社又は非同族会社による完全支配関係を有する法人であること

(b) 業務執行役員（取締役会設置会社の代表取締役及び業務を執行する取締役その他一定の役員をいいます。以下同じ）に対して支給するものであること

(c) 全ての業務執行役員に対して、(d)以降の要件を満たす業績連動給与を

③ In case that director's salary is reduced after three months from the beginning of the fiscal year

The difference between the reduced amount and the amount before the increase is excluded from deductible expense.

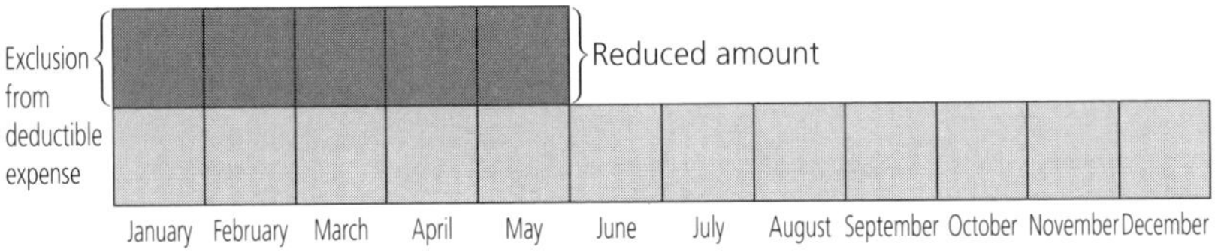

(2) Director's fixed compensation notified in advance

This refers to compensation other than regular fixed remuneration and performance-based compensation that have been notified in advance to the tax office that a fixed amount of salary will be paid to directors at a predetermined time. Compensation may be paid in cash or in the form of shares or stock acquisition rights that meet certain requirements.

The deadline for filing a notification is, in principle, one month from the day on which a director starts his/her duties or four months from the beginning of the fiscal year, whichever comes earlier.

(3) Performance-based compensation

Among performance-based compensation paid in cash and performance-based compensation paid through the issuance of shares or stock acquisition rights, those satisfying the following requirements can be deducted in the calculation of the amount of income of a corporation.

① In the case of payment in cash

(a) The corporation that pays the director's compensation is a non-family company or a corporation with a full control by a non-family company.

(b) The payment shall be made to executive officers (refers to representative directors of a company with board of directors, directors who execute business, and certain other directors; the same shall apply hereinafter.)

支給すること

(d) 客観的な業績連動指標（利益、株価又は売上高）に基づいて交付する金銭の額が決定されること

(e) 確定した額を限度としていること

(f) 交付する金銭の額の算定方法が株式会社の株主総会の決定等の適正な手続きに基づいていること

(g) 交付する金銭の額の算定方法の内容が有価証券報告書で開示されていること

(h) 業績連動指標の確定の日の翌日から１か月以内に支給されること

(i) 支給額を損金経理していること

② 株式又は新株予約権による交付の場合

(a) 役員報酬を支給する法人が非同族会社又は非同族会社による完全支配関係を有する法人であること

(b) 業務執行役員に対して支給するものであること

(c) 全ての業務執行役員に対して、(d)以降の要件を満たす業績連動給与を支給すること

(d) 客観的な業績指標（利益、株価又は売上高）に基づいて交付する株式又は新株予約権の数が決定されること

(e) 確定した数を限度としていること

(f) 交付する株式又は新株予約権の数の算定方法が株式会社の株主総会の決定等の適正な手続きに基づいていること

(g) 交付する株式又は新株予約権の数の算定方法の内容が有価証券報告書で開示されていること

(h) 業績連動指標の確定の日の翌日から２か月以内に支給されること

(i) 支給額を損金経理していること

(j) 株式又は新株予約権による支給の場合、その行使によって上場株式が交付されるものであること

(c) All executive officers shall be provided with performance-based compensation that meets the requirements of (d) and thereafter.
(d) The amount of money to be granted shall be determined based on objective performance indicators (profit, stock price or sales).
(e) The amount is limited to a fixed amount.
(f) The method of calculating the amount of money to be paid is based on appropriate procedures such as decisions at the shareholders' meeting of the Kabushiki Kaisha.
(g) The details of the method of calculating the amount of money to be paid are disclosed in the annual securities report.
(h) The payment shall be made within one month from the day following the date of establishment of the performance-based indicator.
(i) The amount paid is recognized as expenses for accounting purposes.

② In the case of payment through issuance of shares or stock acquisition rights

(a) The corporation that pays the director's compensation is a non-family company or a corporation with a full control by a non-family company.
(b) The payment shall be made to executive officers.
(c) All executive officers shall be provided with performance-based compensation that meets the requirements of (d) and thereafter.
(d) The number of shares or stock acquisition rights to be issued is determined based on objective performance indicators (profit, stock price or sales).
(e) The number is limited to a fixed number.
(f) The method of calculating the number of shares or stock acquisition rights to be issued is based on appropriate procedures such as decisions at the shareholders' meeting of the Kabushiki Kaisha.
(g) The details of the method of calculating the number of shares or stock acquisition rights to be issued are disclosed in the annual securities report.
(h) The payment shall be made within two months from the day following the date of establishment of the performance-based indicator.
(i) The amount paid is recognized as expenses for accounting purposes.
(j) In the case of payment in the form of shares or stock acquisition rights, listed shares shall be issued upon such exercise.

(4) 不相当に高額な役員給与の損金不算入

役員に対して支給する給与が上記(1)から(3)のいずれかの要件を満たすものであっても、次のいずれかの基準に照らして相当とされる金額を超える場合には、その超える部分の金額は損金の額に算入されません。

① 実質基準

役員の職務の内容、その内国法人の収益及びその使用人に対する給与の支給の状況、その内国法人と同種の事業を営む法人でその事業規模が類似するものの役員に対する給与の支給の状況等に照らし、その役員の職務に対する対価として相当であると認められる金額を超える場合におけるその超える部分の金額

② 形式基準

定款の規定又は株主総会等の決議により、役員に対する給与として支給することができる金銭その他の資産について、限度額等を定めている内国法人が、その限度額を超える役員給与を支給している場合のその超える部分の金額

5 寄附金課税

法人税法上の寄附金とは、法人が行った金銭その他の資産又は経済的な利益の贈与又は無償の供与をいいます。法人の行った支出のうち、法人が行う事業活動との関連性が認められないものを寄附金としてその全額を損金としないとする考え方もあり得ますが、現実には事業関連性の区分は困難な場合が多いため、法人税法は損金算入限度額を設け、形式基準により事業関連性を区分するという考え方をとっています。なお、国、地方自治体や財務大臣が指定する一定の団体への寄附金は、国が行う活動を代わりに行ったとも考えられますので、その支出額の全額が法人税法上損金の額に算入されます。また、特定の公益活動を行う法人やNPOなどに支出する寄附金も、損金算入限度額の範囲内であれば、その事業年度の損金の額に算入されます。これら以外に対する寄附金についても、損金算入することは可能ですが、その損金算入限度額は、公益活動

(4) Exclusion of excess remuneration for director

Even if the compensation to be paid to directors meets any of the requirements from (1) to (3) above, if it exceeds the amount deemed reasonable in light of any of the following criteria, the excess amount shall be excluded from deductible expenses.

① Substance criteria

If the amount of compensation exceeds the amount that is considered reasonable as compensation for the duties of the director, by comparing with the details of the duties of the director, the earnings of the domestic corporation and the payment of salaries to its employees, and the payment of compensations to directors of a corporation engaged in the same type of business as the domestic corporation and whose business is similar in size, the amount of such excess.

② Formal criteria

In the case of a domestic corporation that, pursuant to its articles of incorporation or a resolution of its shareholders' meeting, etc., sets a limit on the amount of money or other assets that may be paid as director's compensation, and pays director's compensation that exceed such limit, the amount of such excess.

5 Taxation on expense of contribution or donation

A donation under the Corporation Tax Act is a gift or gratuitous provision of money, other assets or economic benefits made by a corporation. It is possible to consider that expenses incurred by a corporation which are not considered to be related to the business activities conducted by the corporation shall be treated as a donation and not be deductible in full. However, in reality, it is often difficult to classify business-related expenses. Therefore, the Corporation Tax Act sets a deductible limit of donation for tax purposes and classifies business-related expenses based on the format criteria.

Donations to certain organizations designated by the national government, local governments and the Minister of Finance may be considered to have been made on behalf of activities conducted by the national government. Therefore, the total amount of such donations is deductible under the Corporation Tax Act. Donations paid to corporations

を行う法人等に対する寄附金に係るものよりも少なくなります。

法人税法上の寄附金の範囲は、金銭の支出によるものに限られず、経済的な利益の供与を含むなど、社会通念よりも広いものです。経済的な利益の供与のうち、特に以下のものに注意が必要です。

① 債権放棄

法人が有する債権を放棄すると、原則としてその債務者に対して経済的な利益を供与したものとみて、その放棄した債権額は法人税法上寄附金とされます。ただし、その債権放棄をしなければ今後より大きな損失を蒙ることになることが社会通念上明らかであると認められるためやむを得ずその債権放棄をするに至った等そのことについて相当な理由があると認められるときは、その損失負担等により供与する経済的利益の額は、寄附金の額に該当しないものとされます。

② 低廉譲渡

法人がその有する資産を時価よりも低い価額で譲渡したような場合、その受け取った対価の額と時価との差額は寄附金とされます。

③ 国外関連者に対する寄附金

移転価格税制上の国外関連者に対する贈与、低廉譲渡その他の経済的な利益の供与は寄附金とされます。なお、国外関連者に対する寄附金の額は、その全額が損金不算入とされます。

6 同族会社

(1) 同族会社の概要

同族会社とは、3以下の株主（同族株主）グループによってその発行済株式又は議決権の50％超を保有されている会社をいいます。同族会社は、少数の者に支配されていることから、法人の所得金額を恣意的に操作されてしまう可能性を排除できないという趣旨で、法人税法、所得税法及び相続税法において租

engaged in specific public interest activities and NPOs are deductible for the fiscal year as long as they are within the deductible limit of donation. Donations other than those listed above may be deductible, but the deductible limit of donation will be lower than that for donations to corporations engaged in public interest activities.
The scope of donations under the Corporation Tax Act is broader than social norms, including the provision of economic benefits, and is not limited to monetary expenditures. Among the provision of economic benefits, particular attention should be paid to the following:

① Debt waiver

If a corporation renounces a claim, in principle, it is deemed that an economic benefit has been given to the debtor, and the amount of the renounced claim is treated as a donation under the Corporation Tax Act. However, if it is deemed that there are reasonable grounds for the debt waiver, such as unavoidable circumstances where it is deemed that it is obvious from social norms that if the debt is not waived, the corporation will suffer larger losses in the future, the amount of economic benefit to be provided due to the burden of losses, etc. shall not be considered as the amount of the donation.

② Transfer

If a corporation transfers its assets at a price lower than market value, the difference between the amount of consideration received and market value is deemed to be a donation.

③ Donations to foreign affiliates

Gifts, transfers at a price lower than market value, and other economic benefits to foreign affiliates under the transfer pricing taxation system are treated as donations. The full amount of donations to foreign affiliates are excluded from deductible expense.

6 Family company

(1) Outline of the family company

A family company is a company in which more than 50% of its issued shares or voting rights are held by three or fewer groups of shareholders (family shareholders). Since a family company is controlled by a small number of persons, the possibility of arbitrary

税回避を防止するための各種規定が設けられています。

(2) 同族株主

個人も法人も同族株主となり得ます。この個人又は法人と法人税法に定める特殊の関係があると認められる別の個人又は法人も、同族会社の判定をしようとする会社（以下、「判定対象会社」といいます）の株式を保有していると、1つの同族株主グループに含められることになります。特殊の関係の概要は、以下のようになります。

① 特殊の関係（個人の同族株主の場合）

判定対象会社の株主（以下、「判定対象株主」といいます）と次に掲げる関係を有する者が判定対象会社の株式を保有しているときは、これらの者も判定対象株主と1つの同族株主グループを形成するものとして扱われます。

(a) 株主の配偶者、六親等内の血族及び三親等内の姻族
(b) 株主と事実上婚姻関係と同様の事情にある者
(c) 個人株主の使用人
(d) (a)から(c)以外の者で個人株主から受ける金銭その他の資産によって生計を維持しているもの
(e) (b)から(d)に該当する者と生計を一にするこれらの者の親族

② 特殊の関係（法人の同族株主の場合）

(a) 判定対象会社の株主（以下、「判定対象株主」といいます）の1人（その判定対象株主が個人の場合は(2)①の者を含みます）に支配（(3)参照）されている他の会社
(b) 判定対象株主の1人及び(a)の特殊の関係のある会社に支配されている他の会社
(c) 判定対象株主の1人並びに(a)及び(b)の会社に支配されている他の会社

manipulation of corporate income cannot be ruled out. Therefore, various provisions have been established in the Corporation Tax Act, the Income Tax Act, and the Inheritance Tax Act to prevent tax avoidance.

(2) Family shareholder

Both an individual and a corporation can be family shareholders. If another individual or corporation that is deemed to have a special relationship with this individual or corporation under the Corporation Tax Act also holds shares of the company that is about to be determined as a family company (hereinafter referred to as "Company Subject to Determination"), it will be included in one family shareholder group. An outline of a special relationship is as follows.

① Special relationship (in the case of a family shareholder of an individual)

If a person who has any of the following relationships with a shareholder of the Company Subject to Determination (hereinafter referred to as "Shareholders Subject to Determination") holds shares of the Company Subject to Determination, such person is also treated as forming one family shareholder group with the Shareholders Subject to Determination.

(a) A spouse of a shareholder, a relative by blood within the sixth degree of kinship, and in-law within the third degree of kinship
(b) A person who is in a de facto marital relationship with a shareholder
(c) An employee of an individual shareholder
(d) A person other than those listed in (a) through (c) whose livelihood is supported by money or other assets received from an individual shareholder
(e) Relatives of those who make a living with a person who falls under (b) through (d)

② Special relationship (in the case of a family shareholder of a corporation)

(a) Any other company controlled (refer to (3)) by one of the Shareholders Subject to Determination (if the Shareholder Subject to Determination is an individual, the person in (2)① is included)
(b) Any other company controlled by one of the Shareholders Subject to Determination and a company with a special relationship mentioned in (a) above

(3)　支配の意義

(2)②における支配の概要は以下のようになります。

(a) 他の会社の発行済株式又は出資（その有する自己の株式又は出資を除く）の総数又は総額の50％を超える数又は金額の株式又は出資を有する場合

(b) 他の会社の次に掲げる議決権のいずれかにつき、その総数（当該議決権を行使することができない株主等が有する当該議決権の数を除く）の50％を超える数を有する場合

(i) 事業譲渡、解散、組織再編行為又は現物出資に関する決議に係る議決権

(ii) 役員の選任及び解任に関する決議に係る議決権

(iii) 役員の報酬、賞与等についての決議に係る議決権

(iv) 剰余金の配当又は利益の配当に関する決議に係る議決権

(c) 他の会社の株主等の総数の半数を超える数を占める場合

(4)　同族会社に対する特別な規定

同族会社に該当する法人について専ら適用される規定としては、次のようなものがあります。

(a) 使用人兼務役員の範囲の制限

(b) 業績連動給与の損金不算入（非同族会社による完全支配関係がある同族会社を除く）

(c) 行為計算否認

(d) 特定同族会社の留保金課税

(c) Any other company controlled by one of the Shareholders Subject to Determination and companies mentioned in (a) and (b) above

(3) Meaning of control

The outline of control in (2)② is as follows.

(a) In the case of holding shares or capital contributions in a number or amount exceeding 50% of the total number or total amount of issued shares or capital contributions (excluding its own shares or capital contributions) of other companies

(b) As for any of the following voting rights of other companies, in the case of holding a number exceeding 50% of the total number (excluding the number of such voting rights held by shareholders, etc. who cannot exercise such voting rights):

   (i) Voting rights pertaining to resolutions concerning transfer of business, dissolution, reorganization, or contribution in kind

   (ii) Voting rights pertaining to resolutions concerning the appointment and dismissal of officers

   (iii) Voting rights pertaining to resolutions on remuneration, bonuses, etc. of officers

   (iv) Voting rights pertaining to resolutions concerning dividends of surplus or dividends of profits

(c) In the case where the number exceeds half of the total number of shareholders, etc. of other companies

(4) Special provisions for family company

The following provisions apply exclusively to corporations that fall under the category of family company.

(a) Limitations on the scope of employee-director

(b) Exclusion from deductible expense of performance-based compensation (excluding family company with full control by non-family company)

(c) Denial of action or calculation

(d) Taxation on undistributed profit for specific family company

7　完全支配関係と支配関係

(1)　支配関係

支配関係とは、一の者（その者が個人である場合には、その者及びこれと**6**(2)①の特殊の関係のある個人。以下(1)において同じ）が法人の発行済株式等の50％超を直接若しくは間接に保有する関係（以下、「当事者間の支配の関係」といいます）又は一の者との間に当事者間の支配の関係がある法人相互の関係をいうこととされています。

①　当事者間の支配の関係

(a) 一の者が法人の発行済株式の50％超を保有する関係（以下、「直接支配関係」といいます）をいいます。

(b) 次のいずれかに該当する場合も、直接支配関係を有するものとみなされます。

(i) (a)の一の者及びこれとの間に直接支配関係がある1若しくは2以上の法人が他の法人の発行済株式の50％超を保有する場合

(ii) (a)の一の者との間に直接支配関係がある1若しくは2以上の法人が他の法人の発行済株式の50％超を保有する場合

(2)　完全支配関係

完全支配関係とは、次のいずれかの関係をいいます。

(a) 一の者（その者が個人である場合には、その者及びこれと**6**(2)①の特殊の関係のある個人。以下(2)において同じ）が法人の発行済株式等の全部を直接若しくは間接に保有する関係（以下、「当事者間の完全支配の関係」といいます。以下(2)において同じ）

(b) 一の者との間に当事者間の完全支配の関係がある法人相互の関係

7 100% controlling relationship and controlling relationship

(1) Controlling relationship

A controlling relationship refers to a relationship in which a single person (if that person is an individual, that person and an individual with whom that person has special relationship as set forth in 6(2)①; hereinafter the same applies in (1)) directly or indirectly holds more than 50% of the issued shares, etc. of a corporation (hereinafter referred to as "Relationship of Control between the Parties"), or a mutual relationship between corporations that have a Relationship of Control between the Parties with a single person.

① Relationship of Control between the Parties

(a) A relationship in which a single person holds more than 50% of the issued shares of a corporation (hereinafter referred to as "Direct Control Relationship").

(b) It is also considered to have Direct Control Relationship if any of the following applies:

(i) In the case where a single person set forth in (a) and one or more corporations that have Direct Control Relationship with such single person hold more than 50% of the issued shares of another corporation

(ii) In the case where one or more corporations that have Direct Control Relationship with a single person set forth in (a) hold more than 50% of the issued shares of another corporation

(2) 100% controlling relationship

100% controlling relationship means any of the following relationships.

(a) A single person (if that person is an individual, that person and an individual with whom that person has special relationship as set forth in 6(2)①; hereinafter the same applies in (2)) directly or indirectly holds all of the issued shares, etc. of a corporation (hereinafter referred to as "Relationship of Complete Control between the Parties"; hereinafter the same applies in (2))

(b) Mutual relationship of corporations who have Relationship of Complete Control between the Parties with a single person

① 当事者間の完全支配の関係

(a) 一の者が法人の発行済株式の全部を保有する関係（以下、「直接完全支配関係」といいます）をいいます。

(b) 次のいずれかに該当する場合も、直接完全支配関係を有するものとみなされます。

(i) (a)の一の者及びこれとの間に直接完全支配関係がある1若しくは2以上の法人が他の法人の発行済株式等の全部を保有する場合

(ii) (a)一の者との間に直接完全支配関係がある1若しくは2以上の法人が他の法人の発行済株式等の全部を保有する場合

8 中小企業向け特別措置

(1) 中小企業向け特別措置

普通法人のうち、事業年度終了の時において資本金の額又は出資金の額が1億円以下である中小企業は、次のような法人税法上の特別措置の適用を受けることができます。

・法人税率の低減（年800万円までの課税所得について、19％（ただし時限的に15％）。本則は23.2％）

・課税所得の全額を繰越欠損金と相殺可能（本則は課税所得の50％までに制限）

・欠損金の繰戻還付を適用可能（本則は適用停止中）

・法定割合による貸倒引当金の繰入れ可能（本則は実績貸倒率の計算が必要）

・特定同族会社の留保金課税の不適用

・交際費等を年800万円まで損金算入可能（本則は接待飲食費の額の2分の1に相当する金額以外の交際費等は損金不算入）

① Relationship of Complete Control between the Parties

(a) A relationship in which a single person holds all of the issued shares of a corporation (hereinafter referred to as "Direct Complete Control Relationship").

(b) It is also considered to have Direct Complete Control Relationship if any of the following applies:

(i) In the case where a single person set forth in (a) and one or more corporations that have Direct Complete Control Relationship with such single person hold all of the issued shares of another corporation

(ii) In the case where one or more corporations that have Direct Complete Control Relationship with a single person set forth in (a) hold all of the issued shares of another corporation

8 Special measures for small and medium-sized enterprises (SMEs)

(1) Special measures for SMEs

Among ordinary corporations, SMEs with capital or capital contributions of JPY 100 million or less at the end of the fiscal year are eligible for the following special measures under the Corporation Tax Act.

- Reduction in the corporate tax rate (19% (15% for a time period) for taxable profit up to JPY 8 million per year. Regular tax rate is 23.2%)
- All taxable profit can be offset against tax losses carried forward (the original rule limits it to 50% of taxable profit)
- Net loss carry back is applicable (the original rule currently suspends it).
- Allowance for bad debt can be provided at a statutory rate (the original rule requires calculation of the actual bad debt ratio)
- Non-application of taxation on undistributed profit for specific family company
- Entertainment expenses, etc. can be deductible up to JPY 8 million per year (under the original rule, entertainment expenses, etc. other than the amount equivalent to 1/2 of the amount of food and beverage expenses for entertainment are excluded from deductible expense)

(2) 中小企業向け特別措置の適用を受けられない法人

事業年度終了の時において資本金の額又は出資金の額が１億円以下である法人であっても、その法人が次のいずれかに該当するときは、中小企業向けの法人税法上の特別措置を受けることはできません。

① 大法人（資本金の額又は出資金の額が５億円以上である法人をいいます。以下②において同じ）との間にその大法人による完全支配関係がある場合

② 普通法人との間に完全支配関係がある全ての大法人が有する株式及び出資の全部をこれら全ての大法人のうちいずれか一の法人が有するものとみなした場合においてそのいずれか一の法人とその普通法人との間にそのいずれか一の法人による完全支配関係があることとなる場合（①に該当する法人を除きます）

9 支店形態

(1) 支店の態様

現在の日本の国内法における恒久的施設の定義は、2017年版OECDモデル租税条約における恒久的施設とほぼ同じ内容となっており、具体的には以下の３つに分類されます。

(a) 外国法人の国内にある支店、工場その他事業を行う一定の場所

(b) 外国法人の国内にある建設若しくは据え付けの工事又はこれらの指揮監督の役務提供を行う場所

(c) 外国法人が国内に置く自己のために契約を締結する権限のある者

これらの場所が、その外国法人の事業の遂行にとって準備的又は補助的な水準のものである場合には、それぞれに掲げる場所は、その外国法人の恒久的施設に該当しないこととされています。

(2) Corporations not eligible for special measures for SMEs

A corporation whose amount of capital or capital contributions is not more than JPY 100 million at the end of the fiscal year is not eligible for special measures under the Corporation Tax Act for SMEs if it falls under any of the following:

① In the case where there is a 100% controlling relationship with a large corporation (refers to a corporation whose amount of capital or capital contributions is JPY 500 million or more; hereinafter the same shall apply in ② below)

② In the case where all of the shares and capital contributions of an ordinary corporation held by all large corporations that have a 100% controlling relationship with the ordinary corporation are deemed to be held by any one of those large corporations, and there is a 100% controlling relationship by that one large corporation between that one large corporation and the ordinary corporation (excluding a corporation that falls under ① above)

9 Permanent establishment (PE)

(1) Form of PE

The definition of a PE under current Japanese domestic law is almost the same as that in the OECD Model Tax Convention on Income and on Capital: Condensed Version 2017. Specifically, it is classified into the following three categories:

(a) A branch, factory or any other fixed place of business of a foreign corporation located in Japan

(b) A place in Japan where a foreign corporation conducts construction or installation work or provides services for directing and supervising such construction or installation work

(c) A person who is placed in Japan by a foreign corporation and has the authority to conclude contracts on its own behalf

If these places are of a preparatory or auxiliary nature for the execution of the business of the foreign corporation, the places listed in the respective items are not considered to be a PE of the foreign corporation.

	活動の態様	恒久的施設とはならない場所
1	その外国法人に属する物品又は商品の保管、展示又は引渡しのためにのみ施設を使用すること	その施設
2	その外国法人に属する物品又は商品の在庫を保管、展示又は引渡しのためにのみ保有すること	その保有することのみを行う場所
3	その外国法人に属する物品又は商品の在庫を事業を行う他の者による加工のためにのみ保有すること	その保有することのみを行う場所
4	その事業のために物品若しくは商品を購入し、又は情報を収集することのみを目的として、(1)の場所を保有すること	その場所
5	その事業のために前各号に掲げる活動以外の活動を行うことのみを目的として、(1)の場所を保有すること	その場所
6	1から4までに掲げる活動及び当該活動以外の活動を組み合わせた活動を行うことのみを目的として、(1)の場所を保有すること	その場所

なお、外国法人の国内にいる代理人がその外国法人のために行う活動が、その外国法人の事業の遂行にとって準備的又は補助的な性格のものである場合には、その代理人は恒久的施設に該当しないこととされています。

ただし、その本店が所在する国と日本の間で締結された租税条約の恒久的施設に係る定義規定が2017年版OECDモデル租税条約に定める恒久的施設の定義に整合するように改定されていない場合には、引き続きその二国間条約における恒久的施設の定義に基づいて恒久的施設の判定が行われることになります。

(2) 支店に対する課税方式

恒久的施設の所得は、帰属主義によって認識されます。帰属主義とは、外国法人が恒久的施設を通じて事業を行う場合に得る所得は、その恒久的施設が本店等から分離・独立した企業であると擬制した場合にその恒久的施設に帰せられる所得をいうとする考え方をいいます。恒久的施設に帰せられる所得は、そ

	Type of activity	Places that do not become PE
1	Using a facility solely for the purpose of storing, displaying, or delivering the goods or merchandise belonging to the foreign corporation	The facility
2	Holding the inventory of goods or merchandise belonging to the foreign corporation solely for the purpose of storing, displaying, or delivering them	A place where only holding is performed
3	Holding the inventory of goods or merchandise belonging to the foreign corporation solely for the purpose of processing by another person engaged in the business	A place where only holding is performed
4	Holding a facility described in (1) solely for the purpose of purchasing goods or merchandise, or collecting information for the business	That place
5	Holding a facility described in (1) solely for the purpose of conducting activities other than those listed in the preceding items for the business.	That place
6	Holding a facility described in (1) solely for the purpose of conducting a combination of activities listed in 1 through 4 and activities other than those listed in 1 through 4 above.	That place

If the activities conducted by a foreign corporation's agent in Japan for the foreign corporation are preparatory or auxiliary to the foreign corporation's business, such agent is not considered to be a PE.

However, if the definition of a PE in the tax treaty concluded between the country where the head office is located and Japan has not been revised to be consistent with the definition of a PE in the 2017 OECD Model Tax Convention on Income and on Capital, the PE will continue to be determined based on the definition of a PE in the tax treaty.

(2) Taxation system for PE

The income of a PE is recognized on an attributable income approach. The attributable income approach refers to the concept that the income earned by a foreign corporation when it conducts business through a PE is the income attributable to the PE when the PE is assumed to be a company separated and independent from the head office, etc. Income attributable to a PE is to be determined by comprehensively taking into account

の恒久的施設及び本店等が果たす人的機能、負担するリスクや使用する資産等の状況を総合的に勘案して決定することとされています。帰属主義の最大の特徴は、本支店間の内部取引であっても、独立の事業者同士の取引とみなして、収益及び費用を認識する点にあります。日本に恒久的施設を有する外国法人は、内国法人の場合と多くの点で共通するプロセスで課税所得を計算し、法人税及び消費税を申告し、納税を行うこととされています。

(3) 本店配賦経費の取扱い

本店において生じた恒久的施設の運営のための費用を恒久的施設に配賦する場合、その費用はその恒久的施設に帰属する所得の計算上費用とすることができます。ただし、そのためには、その配分の計算の基礎となる以下の書類を保存しておく必要があります。

① 本店配賦経費の配分の基礎となる費用が外国法人の恒久的施設を通じて行う事業及びそれ以外の事業に共通するものであることについての説明、その明細並びにその内容を記載した書類

② 合理的と認められる基準により配分するための計算方法の明細を記載した書類

③ ②の計算方法が合理的であるとする理由を記載した書類

10 国外の関連会社との取引に対する課税の方針

日本の法人税法には、独立企業原則を柱とする移転価格税制が具備されています。このため、関連会社間の取引価格は、「独立企業原則」に基づいて設定される必要があります。「独立企業原則」とは、経済協力開発機構（OECD）の主導により確立された関連会社間の取引に係る国際課税原則です。簡単に言えば、関連会社の間の取引価格は、独立第三者間の取引価格（独立企業間価格）と同様のものでなければならない、とする考え方です。日本の移転価格税制は、法

the people functions performed, risks assumed, and assets used by the PE and the head office, etc. The most distinctive feature of the attributable income approach is that even internal transactions between the head office and branch offices are regarded as transactions between independent business entities and revenue and expenses are recognized. Foreign corporations with PE in Japan are required to calculate their taxable profit through a process that is similar in many respects to that for domestic corporations, and to file and pay corporate tax and consumption tax.

(3) Head office cost allocation

If expenses incurred at the head office for the operation of a PE are allocated to the PE, such expenses may be treated as expenses in calculating the income attributable to the PE. However, to do so, the following documents, which serve as the basis for the calculation of the allocation, must be maintained.

① A document stating an explanation that the expenses which serve as the basis for the allocation of the head office allocated expenses are common to both the business conducted through the PE of the foreign corporation and any other business, and a detailed description thereof, and the contents thereof

② A document stating the details of the method of calculation for the allocation based on standards that are found to be reasonable

③ A document stating the reasons why the calculation method set forth in ② is reasonable

10 Tax policy on transactions with foreign affiliates

The Japanese Corporation Tax Act has a transfer pricing taxation system based on the arm's length principle. Therefore, prices for transactions between affiliates must be set in accordance with the "arm's length principle." The "arm's length principle" is an international tax principle for transactions between affiliates established under the initiative of the OECD. To put it simply, the concept is that the transaction price between affiliates must be the same as the transaction price between independent uncontrolled parties (arm's length price). Transfer pricing taxation in Japan is invoked when a company did

人が国外の関連会社との取引を独立企業間価格で行わなかったことにより、それを独立企業間価格によって行ったとした場合に得られたであろう課税所得と比較して、より少額な課税所得に基づいて申告したと認められる場合に発動します。

not conduct transaction with a foreign affiliate at arm's length price and is therefore considered to have filed profit based on a smaller taxable profit than would have been earned if it had conducted such transaction at arm's length price.

3 所得税

1 納税義務者

(1) 総論

所得税の納税義務者は、個人についていえば、居住者及び非居住者となります。なお、居住者は、非永住者と非永住者以外の居住者に区分されますが、特に断りがない場合は、これらをまとめて居住者とすることもよくあります。居住者と非居住者では、課税される所得の範囲が異なりますので、この分類には重要な意味があります。

区分		課税所得の範囲
居住者		
	非永住者以外の居住者	全世界所得
	非永住者	国内源泉所得及び国内源泉所得以外で日本に送金されたもの
非居住者		国内源泉所得

(2) 居住者

① 居住者とは

所得税法における居住者とは、国内に住所を有し、又は現在まで引き続いて1年以上居所を有する個人をいうものとされています。また、非永住者は、居住者のうち、日本の国籍を有しておらず、かつ、過去10年以内において国内に住所又は居所を有していた期間が合計して5年以下である個人をいうものとされています。非永住者に該当しない居住者は、非永住者以外の居住者とされます。

3 INDIVIDUAL INCOME TAX

1 Taxpayer

(1) General remarks

As for individuals, taxpayers of income tax are classified as residents and non-residents. Residents are classified as non-permanent residents and residents other than non-permanent residents, but unless otherwise specified, they are often collectively referred to as residents. This classification has important implications because the scope of taxable profit is different between residents and non-residents.

Classification		Scope of taxable profit
Resident		
	Residents other than non-permanent residents	Worldwide income
	Non-permanent resident	Domestic source income and income other than domestic source income remitted to Japan
Non-resident		Domestic source income

(2) Resident

① What is resident?

A resident under the Income Tax Act is defined as an individual who has a domicile in Japan or has a continuous residence in Japan for one year or more. A non-permanent resident is a resident who does not have Japanese nationality and has had a domicile or residence in Japan for a total of five years or less within the past ten years. Residents who do not fall under the category of non-permanent residents are considered as residents other than non-permanent residents.

② 住所と居所の意義

ある個人が所得税法上の居住者に該当するかどうかは、その個人が日本国内に住所を有するか、又は１年以上居所を有するかどうかで判断されます。この住所の意義は、各人の生活の本拠をいい、生活の本拠であるかどうかは客観的事実によって判定することとされています。この場合の客観的事実について法律に定めはありませんが、過去の裁判例においては、滞在日数、住居、職業、生計を一にする配偶者その他の親族の居所、資産の所在等を総合的に考慮して判断するとの考え方が示されています。なお、所得税法上の住所判定はあくまで実態に即して行われるものであり、ビザのステータスや住民票の有無により自動的に判定されることはありません。

また、居所とは、その人の生活の本拠ではないが、その人が現実に居住している場所と日本の国税庁により説明されています。つまり、ある個人が住所と言えるほどの場所を日本国内に有していないとしても、日本に１年以上現実に居住していれば、その個人は所得税法上居住者とされます。

③ 居住者の推定

日本に入国した個人が、下記の(a)又は(b)の要件を満たす場合には、居住者と推定される規定が設けられています。

(a) その者が国内において、継続して１年以上居住することを通常必要とする職業を有すること

(b) その者が日本の国籍を有し、かつ、その者が国内において生計を一にする配偶者その他の親族を有することその他国内におけるその者の職業及び資産の有無等の状況に照らし、その者が国内において継続して１年以上居住するものと推測するに足りる事実があること

この推定規定の(a)に関連して、国内において事業を営み若しくは職業に従事するため国内に居住することとなった者は、日本に在留する期間が契約等によりあらかじめ１年未満であることが明らかであると認められる場合を除き、居住者に該当するものとして取り扱われます。この契約等の中には、出張や出

② Meaning of domicile and residence

Whether an individual is a resident under the Income Tax Act is determined by whether the individual has a domicile in Japan or has a residence for one year or more. The meaning of domicile refers to principal place of daily activity and whether it is the principal place of daily activity is to be determined based on objective facts. There is no provision in law regarding objective facts in this case, but in past court cases, it is stated that a judgment should be made by comprehensively taking into account the number of days of stay, residence, occupation, residence of spouse or other relatives who share the same livelihood, and the location of assets. The determination of domicile under the Income Tax Act is based on the actual situation and is not automatically determined based on the status of visa or the existence of certificate of residence.

A residence is not a principal place of daily activity, but it is explained by the National Tax Agency of Japan as the place where the person actually lives. In other words, even if an individual does not have a place in Japan that can be said to be his or her domicile, if he or she has actually lived in Japan for more than one year, he or she is considered a resident under the Income Tax Act.

③ Presumption of resident

There is a provision that an individual who enters Japan is presumed to be a resident if he/she meets the requirements of (a) or (b) below.

(a) The person has an occupation which normally requires him/her to reside in Japan continuously for one year or more

(b) The person has Japanese nationality, has a spouse or other relatives who share the same livelihood in Japan, and in light of the person's occupation and assets in Japan, there is a sufficient fact to infer that the person will reside in Japan for one year or more continuously

In relation to (a) of this presumption provision, an individual who has come to reside in Japan in order to operate a business or engage in an occupation in Japan shall be treated as a resident unless it is clear in advance that the period of stay in Japan is less than one year based on a contract, etc. Since these contracts, etc., are considered to include a letter of appointment for business trip or secondment, it is recommended that such letter of appointment or notice clearly stating the period of business trip or secondment be received in advance.

向の辞令なども含まれるものと考えられますので、出張や出向期間を明示した辞令や通知などをあらかじめ受領しておくことが推奨されます。

④ 居住者の課税所得の範囲

非永住者以外の居住者は、その全世界所得に対して課税されます。したがって、居住者が外国で稼得した所得も、基本的に日本で課税されることになります。なお、居住者は外国税額控除の適用を受けることができますので、これによって外国で課された税との二重課税を排除することになります。

非永住者は、国内源泉所得及び国内源泉所得以外の所得のうち日本に送金されたものが日本での課税所得となります。

(3) 非居住者

① 非居住者とは

非居住者とは、居住者以外の者をいうものとされています。

② 非居住者の推定

日本から出国する個人が、下記の(a)又は(b)の要件を満たす場合には、非居住者であると推定する規定が設けられています。

(a) その者が国外において、継続して1年以上居住することを通常必要とする職業を有すること

(b) その者が外国の国籍を有し又は外国の法令によりその外国に永住する許可を受けており、かつ、その者が国内において生計を一にする配偶者その他の親族を有しないことその他国内におけるその者の職業及び資産の有無等の状況に照らし、その者が再び国内に帰り、主として国内に居住するものと推測するに足りる事実がないこと

この推定規定の(a)に関連して、国外において事業を営み若しくは職業に従事するため国外に居住することとなった個人は、その地における在留期間が契約等によりあらかじめ1年未満であることが明らかであると認められる場合を除き、非居住者に該当するものとして取り扱われます。この契約等の中には、

④ Scope of taxable profit of residents

Residents other than non-permanent residents are taxed on their worldwide income. Therefore, income earned by residents in foreign countries is basically taxed in Japan. As residents are eligible for foreign tax credit, this eliminates double taxation with taxes imposed in the foreign country.

For non-permanent residents, domestic source income and income other than domestic source income remitted to Japan are considered taxable profit in Japan.

(3) Non-resident

① What is non-resident?

A non-resident is defined as a person other than a resident.

② Presumption of non-resident

There is a provision that an individual who departs from Japan is presumed to be a non-resident if he/she meets the requirements of (a) or (b) below.

(a) The person has an occupation which normally requires him/her to reside abroad continuously for one year or more

(b) The person has a foreign nationality or has been granted permission for permanent residence in the foreign country under foreign laws and regulations, and the person does not have a spouse or other relatives who share the same livelihood in Japan or, in light of the status of the occupation and assets of the person in Japan, there is no sufficient fact to presume that the person will return to Japan again and will mainly reside in Japan

In relation to (a) of this presumption provision, an individual who has come to reside outside of Japan in order to operate a business or engage in an occupation outside Japan shall be treated as a non-resident unless it is clear in advance that the period of stay in the place is less than one year based on a contract, etc. Since these contracts, etc., are considered to include a letter of appointment for business trip or secondment, it is recommended that such letter of appointment or notice clearly stating the period of business trip or secondment be received in advance.

③ Scope of taxable profit of non-residents

Non-residents are subject to taxation only on their domestic source income. What constitutes domestic source income is defined in the Income Tax Act.

出張や出向の辞令なども含まれるものと考えられますので、出張や出向期間を明示した辞令や通知などをあらかじめ受領しておくことが推奨されます。

③ 非居住者の課税所得の範囲

非居住者は、その有する国内源泉所得に対してのみ課税されます。何が国内源泉所得であるかは、所得税法に規定されています。

2 給与所得に含まれる経済的利益

「経済的利益」とは、個人が金銭以外の財産やサービスの現物の支給を受け、又は権利を与えられることによって受ける経済的な利益をいいます。個人が会社の役員又は従業員の立場で会社から以下のような経済的利益を受けると、それらの経済的利益はその個人の給与所得とされます。国内で支給される給与は、経済的利益も含め、源泉徴収の対象とされます。

	利益供与行為	経済的利益	経済的利益が生じる場合の具体例
1	物品その他の資産の譲渡を無償又は低い対価で受けた場合	その資産のその時における価額又はその価額とその対価の額との差額に相当する利益	役員、使用人が会社から受ける表彰金品、記念品、食事の提供や補助、自社商品等の提供といった場合
2	土地、家屋その他の資産（金銭を除く）の貸与を無償又は低い対価で受けた場合	通常支払うべき対価の額又はその通常支払うべき対価の額と実際に支払う対価の額との差額に相当する利益	借上社宅等の家賃を会社が負担する場合等
3	金銭の貸付け又は提供を無利息又は通常の利率よりも低い利率で受けた場合	通常の利率により計算した利息の額又はその通常の利率により計算した利息の額と実際に支払う利息の額との差額に相当する利益	役員又は使用人に対し無利息又は低利率で金銭を貸付ける場合

2 Economic benefit included in employment income

"Economic benefit" refers to an economic benefit received by an individual from the receipt of non-monetary property or services in kind, or through the granting of rights. If an individual receives any of the following economic benefits from a company in his/her capacity as an officer or employee of the company, such economic benefits are treated as his/her employment income. Salaries paid in Japan, including economic benefits, are subject to withholding tax.

	Acts of profit-sharing	Economic benefit	Examples of cases where economic benefits arise
1	When goods or other assets are transferred free of charge or at a low consideration	Value of the assets at that time or profit equivalent to the difference between that value and the amount of the consideration	Cases in which officers and employees receive rewards, commemorative gifts, meals and subsidies, and company products, etc. from the company
2	When land, houses, or other assets (excluding money) are leased free of charge or at a low consideration	The amount of consideration normally payable or profit equivalent to the difference between the amount of consideration normally payable and the amount of consideration actually paid	Cases in which the company bears the rent for the company-rented house, etc.
3	When a loan or provision of money is received without interest or at an interest rate lower than the ordinary interest rate	The amount of interest calculated based on the ordinary interest rate or profit equivalent to the difference between the amount of interest calculated based on the ordinary interest rate and the amount of interest actually paid	Cases where money is lent to officers or employees without interest or at a low interest rate

4	2及び3以外の用役の提供を無償又は低い対価で受けた場合	その用役について通常支払うべき対価の額又はその通常支払うべき対価の額と実際に支払う対価の額との差額に相当する利益	役員又は使用人が会社から各種サービス（衣服のクリーニング等）の提供を受ける場合、役員のみが利用できる福利厚生施設の維持管理費を会社が負担する場合等
5	買掛金その他の債務の免除を受けた場合	その免除を受けた金額又は自己の債務を他人が負担した場合における当該負担した金額に相当する利益	役員又は使用人が会社に対する債務の免除を受けた場合、会社が役員又は使用人の債務を代わりに弁済した場合

なお、上記の経済的利益のうち、少額であったり受益者が一定の負担をしている場合には、給与所得とはしないとする取扱いが設けられているものがあります。

3 海外中古建物に係る減価償却費の損益通算制限

(1) 背景

原則として、不動産所得の計算上生じた損失の金額は、総合課税に係る他の所得の金額と相殺することができます。このような相殺は、損益通算と呼ばれます。

日本の所得税法には、中古で取得した建物等の固定資産の耐用年数を簡便的に計算できる制度があり、その制度を活用すればその資産の本来使用可能な年数に比べて相当短い耐用年数を適用できるケースがあります。なお、国外で高額の中古建物（以下「国外中古建物」といいます）を取得した者が、この制度を活用して短い耐用年数を用いて計算される多額の減価償却費によって不動産所得の金額の計算上損失を発生させ、これを給与所得など他の所得と損益通算することで所得税額を圧縮する節税スキームが問題視されていました。しかし、本制度の導入によって、このような節税スキームによる所得税法上のメリットは享受できないようになりました。

4	When services other than those described in 2 and 3 are provided free of charge or at a low consideration.	The amount of consideration normally payable for the services or profit equivalent to the difference between the amount of consideration normally payable and the amount of consideration actually paid	Cases where officers or employees receive various services (such as cleaning of clothes) from the company, or where the company bears the maintenance and management costs of welfare facilities that can be used only by officers
5	When an accounts payable or other obligation is exempted	The amount exempted from payment or profit equivalent to the amount borne in cases where his/her own obligation are borne by the others	Cases where an officer or employee has been released from an obligation to the company or when the company has paid the obligations of an officer or employee on behalf of such officer or employee

Among the above-mentioned economic benefits, some of those that are small in amount or for which beneficiaries bear a certain burden are not treated as employment income.

3 Limitation on the aggregation of profit and loss on depreciation of overseas used buildings

(1) Background

As a general rule, the amount of loss incurred in the calculation of real estate income may be offset against the amount of other income related to comprehensive income taxation. Such offsets are called aggregation of profit and loss.

Under the Japanese Income Tax Act, there is a system whereby the useful life of fixed assets such as used buildings can be easily calculated. If this system is used, there are cases where the useful life is considerably shorter than the actual useful life of the assets. In the past, there was a problem with a tax saving scheme in which a person who has acquired high-priced used buildings outside Japan (hereinafter referred to as "Used Building Outside Japan"), using this system, incurs a loss in calculating the amount of real estate income due to a large amount of depreciation calculated using a short useful life, and then reduces the amount of income tax by aggregating the profit and loss with other income such as employment income. However, the introduction of this system has

(2) 制度内容

個人が国外中古建物から生じる不動産所得を有する場合において、その年分の不動産所得の金額の計算上国外不動産所得の損失の金額があるときは、その国外不動産所得の損失の金額に相当する金額は、不動産所得の金額の計算上生じなかったものとみなされます。

この場合、生じなかったものとみなされる損失の金額は、国外中古建物１物件ごとに計算した不動産所得の損失の金額とその損失を生じた国外中古建物に係る減価償却費の額のうちいずれか小さい金額となります。

なお、本制度の適用を受けた個人がその後対象となった不動産を譲渡した場合には、その譲渡所得の金額の計算上譲渡対価の額から控除することができる取得費（残存簿価）の額に、生じなかったものとみなされた減価償却費の額を加算することとされています。

4 外国親会社からのストック・オプション等の取扱い

(1) ストック・オプション

法人の役員又は従業員等が外国の親会社からストック・オプションを付与された場合、そのストック・オプションは日本では税制非適格ストック・オプションに該当します。税制非適格ストック・オプションについては、そのストック・オプションの権利行使をした日において、その権利行使によって取得した株式のその行使日における時価から払込金額を控除した金額が、その権利行使日の属する年分の給与所得又は退職所得として課税の対象となります。この場合、まだ具体的な金銭の収入がない段階で課税が生じることになりますので注意が必要です。また、その取得した株式を譲渡した場合には、譲渡収入から取得価額（ストック・オプションの権利行使の日における株式の時価）を控除した金額がその譲渡日の属する年分の譲渡所得とされます。

made it impossible to enjoy the benefits of such tax saving scheme under the Income Tax Act.

(2) Outline of the system

In the case where an individual has real estate income arising from Used Building Outside Japan, if there is any amount of loss of foreign real estate income in the calculation of the amount of real estate income for the year, the amount equivalent to the amount of loss of foreign real estate income is deemed not to have occurred in the calculation of the amount of real estate income.

In this case, the amount of loss that is deemed not to have occurred is the smaller of the amount of loss of real estate income calculated for each Used Building Outside Japan or the amount of depreciation of the Used Building Outside Japan that caused the loss.

If an individual to whom this system applies subsequently transfers the subject real estate, the amount of depreciation deemed not to have occurred shall be added to the amount of acquisition costs (residual book value) that can be deducted from the amount of consideration for the transfer in calculating the amount of capital gains.

4 Treatment of stock options, etc. from foreign parent company

(1) Stock option

If an officer or employee of a corporation is granted a stock option by a foreign parent company, such stock option is non-qualified stock option in Japan. With respect to non-qualified stock option, on the date of exercise of the stock options, the amount obtained by deducting the amount to be paid from the market value of the shares acquired by the exercise of the stock options as of the exercise date is taxable as employment income or retirement income for the year to which the exercise date falls. Note that in this case, taxation will occur at a stage where no specific cash flow has yet been received. In addition, if the acquired shares are transferred, the amount obtained by deducting the acquisition cost (the market value of the shares on the date of exercise of stock options) from the transfer income shall be treated as capital gains for the year to which the transfer date belongs.

(2) 譲渡制限付株式等

法人の役員又は従業員が外国の親会社から譲渡制限付株式（リストリクテッド・ストック）やリストリクテッド・ストック・ユニット（以下、「RSU」）、パフォーマンス・シェア（以下、「PS」）といった株式報酬を付与された場合、原則的には、譲渡制限付株式については、その譲渡制限が解除された時、RSUやPSについては株式の交付が確定する条件が成就した日の属する年分の給与所得又は退職所得として課税の対象となります。ただし、譲渡制限付株式やRSU等の付与の方式は一様ではありませんので、契約書に記載された条件を精査したうえで個別に判断する必要があります。

(3) 経済的利益に関する調書の提出

外国親会社等からストック・オプションや譲渡制限付株式、RSU、PSといった経済的利益の供与等を受けた役員又は従業員が勤務する内国法人又は外国法人の国内支店は、「外国親会社等が国内の役員等に供与等をした経済的利益に関する調書」及び合計表をそれらの経済的利益の供与があった日の属する年の翌年3月31日（非居住者のうち、供与等を受けた経済的利益の全部又は一部が国内源泉所得となるものを受けた者に係る調書の場合には、翌年4月30日）までに所轄税務署長に提出する必要があります。

5 源泉徴収のタイミング

日本においては、給与（退職金含む）、一定の役務提供の対価、利子、配当、使用料等の支払を国内において行う場合、その支払者は一定の税率により所得税を源泉徴収し、国に納付する必要があります。この場合の「支払」とは、厳密には、「支払に係る債務の消滅」を意味しています。このため、現金による支払の場合だけでなく、利息の元本への組入れ、債務免除や他の債務との相殺といった場合にも、これらが行われたタイミングで源泉徴収が行われることになります。

(2) Restricted stock, etc.

If an officer or employee of a corporation is granted stock-based compensation such as restricted stocks, restricted stock units (RSU) or performance shares (PS) by a foreign parent company, in principle, the restricted stocks are taxable as employment income or retirement income for the year that includes the date when the restriction on transfer is lifted, and RSU and PS are taxable as employment income or retirement income for the year that includes the date on which the condition to determine the issuance of shares is fulfilled. However, since the method of granting restricted stocks, RSU, etc. is not uniform, it is necessary to make individual judgments after closely examining the conditions stated in the contract.

(3) Submission of report concerning economic benefits

A domestic corporation or a branch of a foreign corporation where an officer or employee who has received economic benefits such as stock options, restricted stocks, RSU or PS from a foreign parent company, etc. works is required to submit a "report of economic benefits provided to domestic officers, etc. by foreign parent company, etc." and a total table to the district director of the competent tax office no later than March 31 of the year following the year in which the economic benefits were provided (or by April 30 of the following year in the case of a report pertaining to a non-resident who has received economic benefits for which all or part of the economic benefits received are domestic source income).

5 Timing of withholding at source

In Japan, when the payment of salary (including retirement allowance), consideration for the provision of certain services, interest, dividends, royalties, etc. is made in Japan, the payer is required to withhold income tax at the prescribed rate and pay it to the government. Strictly speaking, "payment" in this case means "extinguishment of obligation related to payment." Therefore, not only in the case of cash payments but also in the case of incorporation of interest to principal, discharge of indebtedness or offset against other debt, withholding will be made at the timing of such actions.

4 消費税

1 インボイス方式

日本では、1989年の消費税導入当初より、課税事業者は、免税事業者からの仕入についても仕入税額控除をすることができました。こうした消費税の制度は、諸外国と同様に要件を満たした請求書を保存することにより仕入に係る消費税額を控除することができる制度（インボイス制度）に改められ、2023年10月1日から適用されます。

(1) インボイス制度の基本的な仕組み

① インボイスの発行には登録申請が必要

適格請求書（以下、「インボイス」とします）を発行するためには、「適格請求書発行事業者」の登録を納税地の所轄税務署長に対して行う必要があります。登録に要する期間は、e-tax経由で3週間程度、書面提出の場合1か月半程度を要します。適格請求書発行事業者の登録を受けることで、事業者はインボイスを発行することができます。なお、免税事業者はそもそもこの登録を受けることができませんので、免税事業者が適格請求書発行事業者の登録を受けようとする場合には、原則として消費税の課税事業者を選択する必要があります。最終消費者向けに商品やサービスを販売するのみの事業者は、インボイスを発行しませんので、必ずしもこの登録を受ける必要はありません。ただし、事業者が、適格請求書発行事業者としての登録を受けていなくても、消費税法が定める課税事業者に係る他の要件を満たしていれば、その事業者は消費税の課税事業者となりますので注意が必要です。

4 CONSUMPTION TAX

1 Invoice system

In Japan, since the introduction of consumption tax in 1989, taxable businesses have been able to claim purchase tax credit even on the amount of purchase from exempt businesses. This consumption tax system will be changed to a system (invoice system) in which purchase tax can be deductible on condition that invoices meeting certain requirements are stored, as in other countries, which will take effect on October 1, 2023.

(1) Basic structure of the invoice system

① Application for registration is required to issue an invoice

In order to issue a qualified invoice (hereinafter referred to as "Invoice"), it is necessary to register as an "issuer of qualified invoice" with the district director of the competent tax office of the place of tax payment. The period required for registration is approximately three weeks via e-tax, and approximately one month and a half for submission in writing. By being registered as an issuer of qualified invoice, the business operator may issue Invoice. A tax-exempt business operator cannot obtain this registration in the first place. Therefore, when a tax-exempt business operator intends to obtain registration as an issuer of qualified invoice, it is necessary to first select a consumption taxpayer in principle. Businesses that only sell goods or services to end consumers do not issue Invoice and do not necessarily need to register. However, it should be noted that even if a business operator is not registered as an issuer of qualified invoice, if the business operator satisfies other requirements for taxpayer prescribed by the Consumption Tax Act, such business operator will be a consumption taxpayer.

② 仕入税額控除にはインボイスの保存が必要

事業者が行った課税仕入れについて、消費税の税額控除を受けるためには、インボイスを保存する必要があります。このことは、インボイスを発行できる事業者からの仕入（購入）でなければ、仕入を行った事業者において消費税の税額控除を受けられないということを意味します。免税事業者はインボイスを発行できませんので、免税事業者からの仕入について消費税の仕入税額控除を適用できないこととなります。免税事業者のままでは取引先から排除されてしまうリスクもありますので、適格請求書発行事業者として登録を受けるかについて検討する必要があります。

また、新たな取引先と仕入取引を開始する際に、その取引先が適格請求書発行事業者であるかどうかは、国税庁が提供するウェブサイト「適格請求書発行事業者公表サイト」で確認することができます。なお、発行を受けたインボイスの内容が正確であるかどうかについての立証責任はインボイスの受領者側にあることとされていますので、受領したインボイスの記載内容の正確性を十分に確認する必要があります。

③ インボイスの記載事項とインボイスの交付

インボイスには、以下の事項を記載する必要があります。

1	適格請求書発行事業者の氏名又は名称及び登録番号
2	課税資産の譲渡等を行った年月日（課税期間の範囲内で一定の期間内に行った課税資産の譲渡等につきまとめて請求書を作成する場合には、当該一定の期間）
3	課税資産の譲渡等に係る資産又は役務の内容（軽減税率の対象となる場合は、その旨）
4	税抜又は税込の請求金額を税率の異なるごとに区分して合計した金額及び適用税率
5	4に係る消費税の額
6	適格請求書を受領する事業者の氏名又は名称

したがって、適格請求書発行事業者となることを選択した場合には、上記記載事項をもれなく盛り込むために自社の請求書の書式を変更する必要がありま

② Invoice must be retained for purchase tax credit

In order to receive a tax credit for consumption tax on taxable purchases made by business operators, Invoice must be retained. This means that if a purchase is not made from a business operator that can issue Invoice, the business operator that makes the purchase will not be eligible for a tax credit for consumption tax. Since tax-exempt operators cannot issue Invoice, the purchase tax credit of consumption tax cannot be applied to purchases from tax-exempt operators. Tax-exempt operator should consider whether to register as an issuer of qualified invoice, as there is a risk of being excluded from business partners if they remain as a tax-exempt business operator.

When starting a purchase transaction with a new business partner, it is possible to check whether the business partner is an issuer of qualified invoice at the "Announcement Site of Issuers of Qualified Invoice" provided by the National Tax Agency. Since the burden of proving whether the contents of Invoice issued are accurate or not is on the recipient of Invoice, it is necessary to sufficiently confirm the accuracy of the contents of Invoice received.

③ Descriptions and issuance of Invoice

The Invoice must include the following information.

1	Name or title of the issuer of qualified invoice and registration number
2	Date on which the transfer, etc. of taxable assets was carried out (in the case where an invoice is prepared collectively for the transfer, etc. of taxable assets carried out within a fixed period within the taxable period, such fixed period)
3	Details of the assets or services related to the transfer, etc. of taxable assets (indicating that the item is subject to reduced tax rate if applicable)
4	Compensation amount totaled separately by tax rate (excluding or including tax) and applicable tax rate
5	Consumption tax amount pertaining to 4
6	Name or title of the business operator that receives Invoice

If a business operator elects to become an issuer of qualified invoice, it must change the format of its invoice to include all of the above information.

す。

インボイスは、紙だけでなく、電子的な方法によっても交付することができます（電子インボイス）。例えば、電子メールにPDFを添付するような方法も電子インボイスとされます。この他、デジタルインボイス推進協議会（E-Invoice Promotion Association：EIPA）によって、グローバルな標準仕様であるPeppol（Pan European Public Procurement Online）をベースとした日本における電子インボイスの標準仕様の策定及びその普及に向けた取組が現在進行中です。

(2) インターネット等を通じて国外から日本国内にデジタルコンテンツ等を提供している事業者について

国外事業者が日本の法人や個人に対してインターネット等を通じて著作物の提供等を行うことを、電気通信利用役務提供といいます。例えば、国外事業者がクラウドベースのウェブアプリケーションを日本の居住者に提供することは、これに当たります。このような電気通信利用役務提供を行う国外事業者が適格請求書発行事業者として登録を受けると、その国外事業者が提供する電気通信利用役務提供を利用する国内の事業者は、その支払う対価の額を消費税の仕入税額控除の対象とすることができます。もし、国外事業者と同様のサービスを提供する国内事業者が存在する場合、適格請求書発行事業者として登録しておくと、取引から排除されるリスクを減らすことができます。

ただし、この登録を受けることで、国外事業者は、日本国内の取引先にインボイスを発行する義務を負うと共に、自らも日本における消費税の納税義務者として消費税の申告納税義務を負うこととなります。

なお、2023年9月30日現在において「登録国外事業者」として「登録国外事業者名簿」に登録されている国外の事業者は、2023年10月1日に適格請求書発行事業者として登録されたものとみなされます。

Invoice can be issued not only by paper but also by electronic means (electronic invoice). For example, attaching a PDF to an e-mail is also considered an electronic invoice. In addition, the E-Invoice Promotion Association (EIPA) is currently working to establish and promote the standard specifications for electronic invoices in Japan based on Pan European Public Procurement Online (Peppol), which is a global standard.

(2) Business operators that provide digital content, etc. from overseas to Japan via the Internet, etc.

The provision of copyrighted works by foreign business operators to Japanese corporations and individuals via the Internet is called the services provided via electronic and telecommunication networks. For example, the provision of a cloud-based web application to a resident of Japan by a foreign business operator is included in this case. If a foreign business operator that provides such electronic services is registered as an issuer of qualified invoice, a domestic business operator that uses such electronic services provided by the foreign business operator may be entitled to purchase tax credit of consumption tax on the amount of consideration paid. If there is a domestic business operator that provides similar services as a foreign business operator, registering as an issuer of qualified invoice will reduce the risk of being excluded from the transaction.
However, by obtaining this registration, a foreign business operator will be obligated to issue Invoice to its business partners in Japan and will also be obligated to file and pay consumption tax as a taxpayer of consumption tax in Japan.
Foreign companies registered in the “Registered Foreign Businesses List” as “Registered Foreign Business” as of September 30, 2023 are deemed to have been registered as issuers of qualified invoice on October 1, 2023.

5 相続税

1　相続税の課税の方法

相続により財産を取得した個々の相続人が納付すべき相続税の額は、以下のプロセスを経て計算されます。

(1)　課税価格の計算

相続又は遺贈（以下、「相続等」）により財産を取得した者に係る課税価格（各人の課税価格）を個々に計算し、その後、同一の被相続人から相続等により財産を取得した全ての者の相続税の課税価格の合計額を計算します。

各人ごとの相続税の課税価格は、以下のように計算します。

	相続等により取得した財産の価額（非課税財産を除く）
＋	相続等により取得したとみなされる財産の価額（非課税財産を除く）
＋	相続時精算課税適用財産のその贈与時の価額
－	債務及び葬式費用の額
＋	被相続人からの３年以内の贈与財産の価額（贈与税の配偶者控除相当額を除く）
＝	各人の課税価格

なお、課税価格の計算においては、小規模宅地の特例など、相続財産が相続人の生活基盤の維持に不可欠なものであるような場合に、その課税価格を減少させる特例が存在します。

また、債務及び葬式費用の額については、相続人が制限納税義務者である場合には、債務については国内財産に係る債務のうちその制限納税義務者の負担に属する部分に限定され、葬式費用の額は控除することができません。

5 INHERITANCE TAX

1 Method of taxation of inheritance tax

The amount of inheritance tax to be paid by each heir who acquires property through inheritance is calculated through the following process.

(1) Calculation of taxable value

The taxable value (taxable value of each person) of those who acquired property by inheritance or devise (hereinafter referred to as "Inheritance, etc.") is calculated individually, and then the total taxable value of inheritance tax of all those who acquired property by Inheritance, etc. from the same ancestor is calculated.
The taxable value of each person's inheritance tax is calculated as follows.

	Value of property acquired through Inheritance, etc. (excluding non-taxable property)
+	Value of property deemed to have been acquired through Inheritance, etc. (excluding non-taxable property)
+	Value at the time of donation of property subject to settlement of inheritance tax at succession
−	Amount of obligations and funeral expenses
+	Value of property donated from the ancestor within three years (excluding the amount equivalent to the deduction of gift tax for spouse)
=	Each person's taxable value

In calculating the taxable value, special provisions exist to reduce the taxable value such as special provisions for small-scale residential land in cases where the inherited property is essential for the maintenance of the life base of the heir.
In addition, with regard to the amount of obligations and funeral expenses, if the heir is a taxpayer with limitation, the amount of obligations shall be limited to the portion of obligations pertaining to domestic property that is borne by the taxpayer with limitation, and the amount of funeral expenses shall not be deducted.

(2) 相続税の総額の計算

① 遺産に係る基礎控除額

(1)の課税価格の合計額から遺産に係る基礎控除額を控除した残額（課税遺産総額）を基に相続税の総額を計算します。

遺産に係る基礎控除額は、3,000万円＋(600万円×法定相続人の数)により計算されます。この場合の法定相続人は、日本の民法の規定に基づいて決定されます。また、相続を放棄した法定相続人がいるような場合でも、その法定相続人も含めたところで遺産に係る基礎控除額を計算します。

② 法定相続分による課税遺産総額の按分

①で算出された課税遺産総額を法定相続人の数に応じた法定相続分で各相続人に按分します。法定相続分の計算方法は民法に定められており、配偶者に2分の1を割り当て、それ以外の法定相続人に残りの2分の1が均等に割り当てられます。代襲相続人がいる場合でも、代襲相続人は死亡した法定相続人の相続分について割り当てを受けますので、結果的に各法定相続人に割り当てられる相続分に影響はありません。

③ 相続税の税率

②によって各法定相続人に按分された課税遺産総額に基づき、法定相続人ごとの相続税の額を算出します。そして、算出された法定相続人ごとの相続税額を合計して、相続税の合計額を算出します。

相続税の税率は、課税遺産総額が増加するにつれて上昇する累進税率です。以下は具体的な相続税額を算出するために用いられる速算表です。

各人に按分された課税遺産総額	税率	税率を乗じて計算した金額から控除する金額
1,000万円以下	10％	−
3,000万円以下	15％	50万円
5,000万円以下	20％	200万円
1億円以下	30％	700万円
2億円以下	40％	1,700万円

(2) Calculation of the total amount of inheritance tax

① Basic deduction for bequest

The total amount of inheritance tax is calculated based on the amount remaining (total taxable bequest) after deducting the basic deduction for bequest from the total taxable value as described in (1).

The basic deduction for bequest is calculated as JPY 30 million + (JPY 6 million × number of legal heirs). In this case, the legal heir is determined based on the provisions of the Japanese Civil Law. In addition, even if there is a legal heir who has renounced the inheritance, the basic deduction for bequest is calculated by including such legal heir.

② Proration of total taxable bequest by legal share of legacy

The total taxable bequest calculated in ① shall be prorated to each heir in proportion to the legal share of legacy based on the number of legal heirs. The method of calculating the legal share of legacy is stipulated in the Civil Law. One half is allocated to the spouse and the remaining half is equally allocated to the other legal heirs. Even if there is a successor in stirps, the successor in stirps will be allotted the inheritance share of the deceased legal heir. Consequently, there will be no impact on the inheritance share allotted to each legal heir.

③ Inheritance tax rate

The amount of inheritance tax for each legal heir is calculated based on the total taxable bequest prorated to each legal heir according to ②. Then, the total amount of inheritance tax is calculated by adding up the calculated amount of inheritance tax for each legal heir. The rate of inheritance tax is a progressive tax rate that increases as the total taxable bequest increases. Below is a quick calculation table used to calculate the specific amount of inheritance tax.

Total taxable bequest prorated to each person	Tax rate	Amount to be deducted from the amount calculated by multiplying the tax rate
JPY 10 million or less	10%	-
JPY 30 million or less	15%	JPY 500,000
JPY 50 million or less	20%	JPY 2 million
JPY 100 million or less	30%	JPY 7 million
JPY 200 million or less	40%	JPY 17 million
JPY 300 million or less	45%	JPY 27 million
JPY 600 million or less	50%	JPY 42 million
Over JPY 600 million	55%	JPY 72 million

3 億円以下	45 %	2,700 万円
6 億円以下	50 %	4,200 万円
6 億円超	55 %	7,200 万円

(3) 各人の算出税額の計算

(2)で計算された相続税の総額を各人が現実に取得した財産の額の割合に応じて配分し、各人の算出税額を計算します。

(4) 各人の納付すべき相続税額の計算

(3)で計算された各人の算出税額に必要に応じて加算すべき金額がある場合にはその金額を加算し、各人に応じた各種の税額控除額を控除して、各人の納付すべき税額を計算します。この段階では、以下の点に注意が必要です。

① 相続税額の加算

被相続人の一親等血族以外の者（被相続人の養子となった被相続人の直系卑属を含み、被相続人の配偶者を除く）については、算出税額について 20 %が加算されます。

② 各種控除

算出税額（加算額がある場合は加算後の金額）からは、以下の税額控除の適用を受けることができます。

控除の種類	内容
暦年課税分の贈与税額控除	相続等により財産を取得した者がその相続開始前 3 年以内に被相続人からその財産の贈与を受けた場合、その財産につき課された贈与税を相続税額から控除できます。
配偶者に対する相続税額の減額	被相続人の配偶者が実際に取得した正味の財産額が、法定相続分と 1 億 6 千万円のいずれか多い金額まで、相続税が免除されます。
未成年者控除	被相続人の法定相続人で 18 歳未満の者が相続等により財産を取得した場合に、相続税額につき一定の控除を受けることができます。

(3) Calculation of the amount of calculated tax for each person

The total amount of inheritance tax calculated in (2) is distributed in proportion to the amount of property actually acquired by each person to calculate the tax amount for each person.

(4) Calculation of the amount of inheritance tax payable by each person

The amount of tax liability by each person is calculated by adding the amount to be added to the amount of tax calculated for each person in (3), if any, and deducting the various tax credits for each person. At this stage, the following points should be noted.

① Addition of inheritance tax

For persons other than first degree blood relatives of the ancestor (including a lineal descendant of the ancestor who was adopted by the ancestor, but excluding the ancestor's spouse), 20% will be added to the calculated tax amount.

② Various deductions

The following tax credit can be applied against the calculated tax amount (or amount after the addition, if any).

Type of deduction	Details
Gift tax credit for calendar year taxation	If a person who has acquired property by Inheritance, etc. receives a gift of the property from the ancestor within three years before the commencement of inheritance, the gift tax imposed on the property may be deducted from the inheritance tax amount.
Reduction of inheritance tax for spouse	The spouse of the ancestor will be exempted from inheritance tax up to the amount of the legal share of legacy or JPY 160 million, whichever is larger.
Tax credit for minor	If a legal heir of the ancestor who is under the age of 18 acquires property due to Inheritance, etc., he/she is eligible for a certain amount of deduction for inheritance tax.
Exemption for persons with disabilities	If a legal heir of the ancestor with a disability under the age of 85 acquires property due to Inheritance, etc., he/she is eligible for a certain amount of deduction for inheritance tax.
Deduction for successive inheritance	If two or more inheritances occur within 10 years, such heir is entitled to a certain amount of deduction for inheritance tax.

障害者控除	被相続人の法定相続人で85歳未満の障害者が相続等により財産を取得した場合に、相続税額につき一定の控除を受けることができます。
相次相続控除	10年以内に2回以上の相続が発生した場合、その相続人は相続税額につき一定の控除を受けることができます。
外国税額控除	相続等により取得した在外財産につき日本の相続税に相当する税が課された場合に、その税額を日本の相続税額から控除します。
相続時精算課税の適用を受けた贈与に係る贈与税額の控除	相続時精算課税制度の適用を受けて納付した贈与税額は、相続税額から控除することができます。

2 納税義務者

相続税及び贈与税の納税義務者の区分は概ね下の表のとおりとなります（特定納税義務者は除きます）。

<table>
<tr><td colspan="3" rowspan="3">相続人・受遺者・受贈者
被相続人
贈与者</td><td colspan="2">日本国内に住所あり</td><td colspan="3">日本国内に住所なし</td></tr>
<tr><td rowspan="2"></td><td rowspan="2">一時居住者(＊1)</td><td colspan="2">日本国籍あり</td><td rowspan="2">日本国籍なし</td></tr>
<tr><td>相続開始前10年以内に住所あり</td><td>相続開始前10年以内に住所なし</td></tr>
<tr><td colspan="3">日本国内に住所あり</td><td></td><td></td><td></td><td></td><td></td></tr>
<tr><td></td><td colspan="2">外国人被相続人(＊2)
外国人贈与者(＊2)</td><td></td><td>居住制限納税義務者</td><td></td><td colspan="2">非居住制限納税義務者</td></tr>
<tr><td rowspan="3">日本国内に住所なし</td><td colspan="2">相続開始前10年以内に住所あり</td><td colspan="2">居住無制限納税義務者</td><td colspan="2">非居住無制限納税義務者</td><td></td></tr>
<tr><td></td><td>非居住被相続人(＊3)
非居住贈与者(＊3)</td><td></td><td rowspan="2">居住制限納税義務者</td><td></td><td colspan="2" rowspan="2">非居住制限納税義務者</td></tr>
<tr><td colspan="2">相続開始前10年以内に住所無し</td><td></td><td></td></tr>
</table>

（＊1）出入国管理及び難民認定法別表第1の在留資格で滞在している者で、相続の開始前15年以内において日本国内に住所を有していた期間の合計が10年以下の者
（＊2）出入国管理法及び難民認定法別表第1の在留資格で滞在している者
（＊3）日本国内に住所を有していた期間、日本国籍を有していない者
（出典：税務大学校講本「相続税法 令和4年度版」9頁）

Foreign tax credit	If a tax equivalent to Japanese inheritance tax is imposed on overseas property acquired through Inheritance, etc., such tax amount may be deducted from the amount of Japanese inheritance tax.
Gift tax credit related to gifts to which taxation on settlement of inheritance tax at succession was applied	The amount of gift tax paid under the taxation system for settlement of inheritance tax at succession can be deducted from the amount of inheritance tax.

2 Taxpayer

The classification of persons liable to pay inheritance tax and gift tax is generally as shown in the table below (excluding specified taxpayer).

<table>
<tr><th colspan="2" rowspan="3">Heir/Devisee/Donee
Ancestor Donor</th><th colspan="2">Domicile in Japan</th><th colspan="3">No domicile in Japan</th></tr>
<tr><th rowspan="2"></th><th rowspan="2">Temporary resident *1</th><th colspan="2">Japanese nationality</th><th rowspan="2">No Japanese nationality</th></tr>
<tr><th>Domiciled in Japan within 10 years prior to commencement of inheritance</th><th>No domicile in Japan within 10 years prior to commencement of inheritance</th></tr>
<tr><td colspan="2">Domicile in Japan</td><td></td><td></td><td></td><td></td><td></td></tr>
<tr><td></td><td>Alien ancestor *2
Alien donor *2</td><td></td><td>Resident taxpayer with limitation</td><td></td><td colspan="2">Non-resident taxpayer with limitation</td></tr>
<tr><td rowspan="3">No domicile in Japan</td><td>Domiciled in Japan within 10 years prior to commencement of inheritance</td><td colspan="2">Resident taxpayer without limitation</td><td colspan="2">Non-resident taxpayer without limitation</td><td></td></tr>
<tr><td>Non-resident ancestor *3
Non-resident donor *3</td><td></td><td rowspan="2">Resident taxpayer with limitation</td><td></td><td colspan="2" rowspan="2">Non-resident taxpayer with limitation</td></tr>
<tr><td>No domicile in Japan within 10 years prior to commencement of inheritance</td><td></td><td></td></tr>
</table>

*1 A person residing under the status of residence listed in Appended Table 1 of the Immigration Control and Refugee Recognition Act who has had a domicile in Japan for a total of 10 years or less within 15 years prior to the commencement of inheritance
*2 A person who is staying under the status of residence listed in Appended Table 1 of the Immigration Control Act and Refugee Recognition Act
*3 A person who does not have Japanese nationality for the period during which he/she was domiciled in Japan
(Source: Page 9 of "Inheritance Tax Act, 2022 Edition", National Tax College textbook)

非居住者が絡む相続における相続税・贈与税の納税義務者の判定において注意すべき点は、相続人・受贈者の状況だけでなく、被相続人・贈与者の状況も加味したところで納税義務の有無とその種類が決定されるということです。特に、相続人・受贈者が日本に一度も来たことがない場合であっても、被相続人が日本に一定期間居住しており、かつ日本国内に財産があると、その相続人は、その取得する国内財産については相続税、贈与税の納税義務を有することとなりますので、注意が必要です。

なお、それぞれの納税義務者の種類ごとの課税財産の範囲は以下の通りとなります。

納税義務者の種類	課税財産の範囲
居住無制限納税義務者	取得財産の全部
非居住無制限納税義務者	取得財産の全部
居住制限納税義務者	日本国内にある財産のみ
非居住制限納税義務者	日本国内にある財産のみ

3 相続税の課税財産

(1) 本来の相続財産

相続税の課税財産は、被相続人の財産に属した権利及び義務（被相続人の一身に専属したものを除きます）で、民法に規定する相続又は遺贈によって相続人が取得したものです。ここでいう財産とは、金銭に見積ることができる経済的価値のあるすべてのものをいいます。

(2) みなし相続財産

法律的に見れば相続等による財産又は経済的な利益の取得に該当しないものであっても、その財産又は経済的な利益の取得が実質的に相続等と同様と認められるものについては、相続等があったものとみなして、その財産又は経済的

In inheritance involving non-residents, the point to be noted in determining who is liable to pay inheritance tax and gift tax is that the existence of tax liability and the scope of taxable property are determined by taking into account not only the status of the heir or donee but also the status of the ancestor or donor. In particular, even if the heir or donee has never been to Japan, if the ancestor has resided in Japan for a certain period of time and has property in Japan, such hair is liable to pay inheritance tax and gift tax on the domestic property acquired by the ancestor.

The scope of taxable property for each type of taxpayer is as follows.

Type of taxpayer	Scope of taxable property
Resident taxpayer without limitation	All of the acquired property
Non-resident taxpayer without limitation	All of the acquired property
Resident taxpayer with limitation	Property located in Japan only
Non-resident taxpayer with limitation	Property located in Japan only

3 Taxable property of inheritance tax

(1) Original inherited property

Properties subject to inheritance tax are the rights and obligations that belong to the properties of the ancestor (excluding those exclusively assigned to the ancestor) and acquired by the heir through inheritance or devise as provided for in the Civil Law. The term "property" as used herein refers to anything with economic value that can be estimated in terms of money.

(2) Deemed inherited properties

Even if the acquisition of property or economic benefit does not legally fall under the category of acquisition of property or economic benefit by Inheritance, etc., if the acquisition of property or economic benefit is deemed to be substantially the same as Inheritance, etc., it shall be deemed that the Inheritance, etc. has occurred and the value of the property or economic benefit shall be included in the taxable property of inheritance tax.

The main properties and their outline are as follows.

な利益の価額を相続税の課税財産に算入します。対象となる主な財産及びその概要は下表のとおりです。

財産・利益の種類	概要
生命保険金等	被相続人の死亡等の保険事故の発生により相続人が取得した保険金について、被相続人が保険料を全部又は一部負担している場合には、その保険金のうち被相続人が負担した保険料の額に対応する部分をその相続人が相続等により取得したものとみなされます。
退職手当金	被相続人の死亡により、その被相続人に支給されるべきであった退職手当金、功労金その他これらに準ずる一定の給与で被相続人の死亡後３年以内に支給が確定したものが相続人に支給された場合、その支給された退職手当金等はその相続人が相続等により取得したものとみなされます。
生命保険契約に関する権利	相続開始時までに保険事故が発生していない生命保険契約で、被相続人が保険料を全部又は一部負担し、かつ、被相続人以外の者が契約者であるものについては、その契約に係る権利のうち被相続人が負担した保険料の額に対応する部分をその契約者が相続等により取得したものとみなされます。
定期金に関する権利	相続開始時までに定期金給付事由が発生していない定期給付金契約で、被相続人が掛金を全部又は一部負担し、かつ、被相続人以外の者が契約者であるものについては、その契約に係る権利のうち被相続人が負担した掛金の額に対応する部分をその契約者が相続等により取得したものとみなされます。
財産の低額譲受による利益	遺言により著しく低い対価の額で財産を譲り受けた者は、その対価の額とその財産の価額との差額に相当する金額を遺贈により取得したものとみなされます。
債務免除等による利益	遺言により対価を支払わず、又は著しく低い対価の額で債務免除、債務引受け又は第三者弁済によって利益を得た者は、その債務免除等を受けた金額を遺贈により取得したものとみなされます。
その他の利益	遺言により無償又は著しく低い価額の対価で利益を受けた者は、その利益を受けた時に、その利益の価額又はその利益の価額から支払った対価の額を控除した金額を遺贈により取得したものとみなされます。
信託に関する権利	適正な対価を支払うことなく信託の受益者等となった場合等には、その受益者等は、その信託に係る権利を相続等により取得したものとみなされます。

Type of properties and interests	Outline
Life insurance claims, etc.	If the ancestor bears all or part of the insurance premiums for the insurance claims obtained by an heir due to the occurrence of an insured event such as the death of the ancestor, the heir is deemed to have acquired the portion of the insurance claims corresponding to the amount of the insurance premiums borne by the ancestor due to Inheritance, etc.
Retirement allowance	Upon the death of an ancestor, if a retirement allowance, merit bonus or certain other salaries equivalent thereto which should have been paid to the ancestor and which has been determined to be paid within three years after the death of the ancestor, is paid to the heir, the retirement allowance, etc. paid will be deemed to have been acquired by the heir due to Inheritance, etc.
Right pertaining to life insurance contract	With respect to life insurance contract for which an insured event has not occurred by the time of commencement of inheritance, where the ancestor bears all or part of the insurance premiums and a person other than the ancestor is the policyholder, the portion of the rights pertaining to the contract corresponding to the amount of insurance premiums borne by the ancestor shall be deemed to have been acquired by the policyholder due to Inheritance, etc.
Right pertaining to periodic payment	In the case of a periodic payment benefit contract for which the grounds for periodic benefit payment have not occurred by the time of commencement of inheritance, if the ancestor bears all or part of the premiums and a person other than the ancestor is the policyholder, the portion of the rights pertaining to the contract corresponding to the amount of the premiums borne by the ancestor shall be deemed to have been acquired by the policyholder due to Inheritance, etc.
Benefit from low value transfer of property	A person who receives a property at a remarkably low value in accordance with a will shall be deemed to have received an amount equivalent to the difference between the amount of such consideration and the value of the property by way of a devise.
Benefit from discharge of indebtedness	In accordance with a will, a person who does not pay the consideration or who has obtained a benefit by discharge of indebtedness with a remarkably low value, debt assumption or third-party performance shall be deemed to have obtained the amount of discharge of indebtedness, etc. by way of a devise.
Other benefit	A person who receives a benefit free of charge or at a remarkably low value according to a will shall be deemed to have acquired the value of the benefit or the amount obtained by deducting the amount of the consideration paid from the value of the benefit by way of a devise at the time of receiving the benefit.

(3) 非課税財産

相続税法に定められた一定の財産については、相続税の課税価格に算入することを要しないこととされています。一定の財産とは、例えば以下のようなものがあります。

① 墓所、霊廟及び祭具並びにこれらに準ずるもの

② 相続人が取得した生命保険金等のうち一定の金額

③ 相続人が取得した退職手当金等のうち一定の金額

4 財産の所在地

居住制限納税義務者や非居住制限納税義務者にとって、相続や贈与によって取得する財産の所在地が日本国内とされるか否かは、重要な問題です。日本の相続税法では、財産の所在地について、以下のような定め（抜粋）を置いています。

財産の種類	財産が所在することとされる場所
動産若しくは不動産又は不動産の上に存する権利	その動産又は不動産の所在
船舶又は航空機	船籍又は航空機の登録をした機関の所在
金融機関に対する預金、貯金、積立金等	これらの受け入れをした営業所又は事務所の所在地
生命保険契約又は損害保険契約の保険金	保険の契約に係る保険会社の本店又は主たる事務所の所在（日本国内に本店又は主たる事務所がない場合において、日本国内にその保険の契約に係る事務を行う営業所、事務所その他これらに準ずるものを有するときにあっては、その営業所、事務所その他これに準ずるものの所在）
退職手当金、功労金その他これらに準ずる給与	その給与を支払った者の住所又は本店若しくは主たる事務所の所在
貸付金債権	債務者の住所又は本店若しくは主たる事務所の所在

Right pertaining to trust	If a person becomes a beneficiary, etc. of a trust without paying proper consideration, he/she is deemed to have acquired the rights pertaining to the trust by Inheritance, etc.

(3) Non-taxable property

Certain properties stipulated in the Inheritance Tax Act are not required to be included in the taxable value of inheritance tax. Certain properties include, for example, the following:

① Graves, mausoleums, ritual equipment, and their equivalents
② A certain amount of life insurance claims, etc. acquired by the heir
③ A certain amount of retirement allowance, etc. acquired by the heir

4 Place of property

For a resident or non-resident taxpayer with limitation, it is an important issue whether the property acquired by inheritance or donation is located in Japan or not.

The Inheritance Tax Act of Japan provides for the location of properties as follows (excerpt):

Type of property	The place where the property is to be located
Movable or immovable property or any right on immovable property	Location of the movable or immovable property
Vessel or aircraft	Location of the organization where the vessel or aircraft is registered
Deposits, savings, reserves, etc. with financial institutions	Location of the business office or place of office that accepted them
Insurance claims under a life insurance contract or non-life insurance contract	Location of the head office or principal office of the insurance company pertaining to the contract for insurance (however, if the insurance company has no head office or principal office in Japan, and has a business office, place of office or any other equivalent place to carry out affairs pertaining to insurance contracts in Japan, the location of such business office or place of business or any other equivalent place)

社債若しくは株式、法人に対する出資又は外国預託証券	社債若しくは株式の発行法人、その出資を受けている法人の本店又は主たる事務所の所在
集団投資信託又は法人課税信託に関する権利	これらの信託の引き受けをした営業所又は事務所等の所在
特許権等若しくはその実施権で登録されているもの又は商標権等若しくはその利用権で登録されているもの	その登録をした機関の所在
著作権、出版権等でこれらの権利の目的物が発行されているもの	これを発行する営業所又は事業所の所在
贈与又は遺贈により取得したとみなされる金銭で低額譲受に係るもの	そのみなされる基因となった財産の種類に応じて本表に掲げる場所。
上記に掲げる財産以外の財産で、営業所又は事業所を有する者のその営業所又は事業所に係る営業上又は事業上の権利	その営業所又は事業所の所在
国債又は地方債	国債又は地方債は国内にあるものとし、外国又は外国の地方公共団体その他これに準ずるものの発行する公債は、その外国にあるものとされる。
上記以外の財産	その財産の権利者であった被相続人又は贈与をした者の住所の所在

なお、日本とアメリカの間で締結されている日米相続税条約においては、上記と異なる定めがありますので、日本とアメリカの相続案件では、この条約の定めに従って資産の所在を判断することになります。

Retirement allowance, merit bonus and other remuneration equivalent thereto	The address or location of the head office or principal office of the person who has paid the remuneration
Loan receivables	The address or location of the head office or office of the debtor
Corporate bonds or shares, contributions to a corporation, or foreign depository receipts	Location of the head office or principal office of the corporation issuing the corporate bonds or shares, or of the corporation receiving the contribution thereof
Rights concerning collective investment trusts or trusts subject to corporate tax	Location of the business office or place of business, etc. which has accepted the trust
Registered patent right, etc. or a license thereof, or registered trademark right, etc. or a right to use thereof.	Location of the organization which has registered them
Copyrights, publication rights, etc. for which the subject matter of such rights has been issued	Location of the business office or place of business issuing them
Money deemed to have been acquired through a gift or devise by way of a low-value transfer	The place specified in this Schedule according to the kind of property which is deemed to be the cause thereof
Any property other than those listed above, which is an operational or business right pertaining to a business office or place of business of a person who has such business office or place of business	Location of its business office or place of business
Government bonds or Japanese municipal bonds	Government bonds or Japanese municipal bonds shall be deemed to be located in Japan, and public bonds issued by a foreign state, a local government of a foreign state, or any other entity equivalent thereto are deemed to be located in that foreign state
Property other than the above	Location of the address of the ancestor or donor who was the right holder of the property

The Japan-U.S. Estate Tax Treaty concluded between Japan and the United States has different provisions from the above. Therefore, in inheritance cases between Japan and the United States, the location of assets shall be determined in accordance with the provisions of the said Treaty.

6 贈与税

1 贈与の内容

(1) 贈与の意義

贈与は、当事者の一方がある財産を無償で相手方に与えるという意思表示をし、その相手方がこれを受諾することによって成立する片務契約です。贈与には、書面によるものと書面によらないものとがあり、書面による贈与については解除はできませんが、書面によらない贈与については、未履行の部分については、いつでも解除することができます。

(2) 贈与の時期

贈与の時期は、それぞれ以下のように定められています。

書面による贈与	その贈与契約の効力が発生した時
書面によらない贈与	その贈与の履行があった時
停止条件付の贈与	その条件の成就の時

2 贈与税の課税財産

(1) 本来の贈与財産

個人が贈与契約によって他の個人から取得した財産は、本来の贈与財産と呼ばれます。ここにいう財産とは、金銭に見積ることができる経済的価値のあるすべてのものをいいます。

6 GIFT TAX

1 Contents of gifts

(1) Meaning of gift

A gift is a one-sided contract that is concluded when one of the parties expresses its intention to give a certain property to the other party free of charge and the other party accepts the gift. There are written and non-written gifts. A written gift cannot be cancelled, but a non-written gift may be cancelled at any time for any unexecuted portion.

(2) Timing of gifts

The timing of each gift is defined as follows.

Gift in writing	At the time when the gift contract becomes effective
Gift not in writing	At the time of execution of the gift
Gift with a condition precedent	At the time of fulfillment of the condition

2 Taxable property of gift tax

(1) Original gifted property

A property acquired by an individual from another individual through a gift contract is referred to as original gifted property. The term “property” as used herein refers to anything with economic value that can be estimated in terms of money.

(2) みなし贈与財産

法律的に見れば贈与による財産又は経済的な利益の取得に該当しないものであっても、その財産又は経済的な利益の取得が実質的に贈与と同様と認められるものについては、贈与があったものとみなして、その財産又は経済的な利益の価額を贈与税の課税財産に算入します。対象となる財産及びその概要は下表のとおりです。

財産・利益の種類	概要
生命保険金等	保険事故の発生により保険金を取得した者が、その保険金に係る保険料を負担していない場合、その保険金を取得した者は、その保険金のうちその者が保険料を負担していないとされる部分を贈与により取得したものとみなされます。
定期金に関する権利	定期金給付契約の給付事由の発生により定期金を取得した者が、その給付金に係る掛金等を負担していない場合、その給付金を取得した者は、その給付金のうちその者が掛金等を負担していないとされる部分を贈与により取得したものとみなされます。
財産の低額譲受による利益	著しく低い対価の額で財産を譲り受けた者は、その譲り受けの時において、その対価の額とその財産の価額との差額に相当する金額を贈与により取得したものとみなされます。
債務免除等による利益	対価を支払わず、又は著しく低い対価の額で債務免除、債務引受け又は第三者弁済によって利益を得た者は、その利益を受けた時に、その債務免除等を受けた金額を贈与により取得したものとみなされます。
その他の利益	無償又は著しく低い価額の対価で利益を受けた者は、その利益を受けた時に、その利益の価額又はその利益の価額から支払った対価の額を控除した金額を贈与により取得したものとみなされます。
信託に関する権利	適正な対価を支払うことなく信託の受益者等となった場合等には、その信託に係る権利を贈与により取得したものとみなされます。

(2) Deemed gift

Even if the acquisition of property or economic benefit does not legally fall under the category of acquisition of property or economic benefit by gift, if the acquisition of property or economic benefit is deemed to be substantially the same as that of gift, it shall be deemed that the gift has occurred and the value of the property or economic benefit shall be included in the taxable property of gift tax. The main properties and their outline are as follows.

Type of properties and interests	Outline
Life insurance claims, etc.	If a person who has acquired an insurance claim due to the occurrence of an insured event does not bear the insurance premium for the insurance claim, the person who has acquired the insurance claim is deemed to have acquired the portion of the insurance claim that the person does not bear the insurance premium by gift.
Right pertaining to periodic payment	If a person who has acquired a periodic payment due to the occurrence of a reason for payment under a periodic payment benefit contract does not bear the premiums, etc. pertaining to the benefit, the person who has acquired the benefit is deemed to have acquired the portion of the benefit that the person does not bear the premiums, etc. by gift.
Benefit from low value transfer of property	A person who receives a property at a remarkably low value of consideration shall be deemed to have received an amount equivalent to the difference between the amount of such consideration and the value of the property by gift at the time of receiving the property.
Benefit from discharge of indebtedness	A person who does not pay the consideration or who has obtained a benefit by discharge of indebtedness with a remarkably low value, debt assumption or third-party performance shall be deemed to have obtained the amount of discharge of indebtedness, etc. by gift at the time of receiving the benefit.
Other benefit	A person who receives a benefit free of charge or at a remarkably low value shall be deemed to have acquired the value of the benefit or the amount obtained by deducting the amount of the consideration paid from the value of the benefit by gift at the time of receiving the benefit.
Right pertaining to trust	If a person becomes a beneficiary, etc. of a trust without paying proper consideration, he/she is deemed to have acquired the rights pertaining to the trust by gift.

(3) 非課税財産

相続税法に定められた一定の財産については、贈与税の課税価格に算入することを要しないこととされています。一定の財産とは、例えば以下のようなものがあります。

(1) 法人からの贈与により取得した財産（ただし、受贈者は、一時所得を取得したものとして所得税が課されます）

(2) 扶養義務者相互間において生活費又は教育費に充てるためにした贈与により取得した財産のうち通常必要と認められるもの

(3) 社交上の香典や贈答品などその取得が贈与に該当するもので、社会通念上相当と認められるもの

3 贈与税の課税価格と控除

贈与税の課税価格は、（本来の贈与財産＋みなし贈与財産－非課税財産）により算出します。また、課税価格からは配偶者控除及び基礎控除の金額を控除することができます。贈与税の課税価格は、暦年ごとに計算します。贈与税の基礎控除は贈与のあった各年において受けることができます。

贈与税の配偶者控除は、国内の居住用不動産又はその取得資金の贈与について、2,000万円を限度に課税価格から控除することができる制度です。なお、適用に当たっては、その贈与を受けた年の翌年3月15日までに受贈者がその贈与を受けた国内の居住用不動産に居住し、かつその後も居住する見込みであること、贈与税の申告書の提出など一定の要件が課されています。

4 贈与税の税額

贈与税の税率は超過累進税率であり、その適用税率は基礎控除後の課税価格に応じて以下のとおりとなります。

(3) Non-taxable property

Certain properties stipulated in the Inheritance Tax Act are not required to be included in the taxable value of gift tax. Certain properties include, for example, the following:

(1) Property acquired through gift from a corporation (however, the donee is subject to income tax as if he/she acquired temporary income.)

(2) Among the properties acquired by gift made between persons under duty to support for the purpose of allocating them for living expenses or education expenses, those that are normally considered necessary

(3) Gifts, such as social condolence money and gifts, whose acquisition is considered to be appropriate in terms of social conventions

3 Taxable value of gift tax and deduction

The taxable value of gift tax is calculated as (original gifted property + deemed gift - non-taxable property). In addition, the amount of exemption for spouse and basic exemption can be deducted from the taxable value. The taxable value of gift tax is calculated for each calendar year. The basic exemption for gift tax is available in each year in which the gift was made.

The exemption of gift tax for spouse is a system that allows a deduction of up to JPY 20 million from the taxable value for a gift of residential real estate in Japan or funds for the acquisition of such real estate. For application, certain requirements are imposed such as that the donee will reside in the gifted residential real estate in Japan by March 15 of the year following the year in which he/she received the gift and is expected to reside thereafter, and that he/she will file a tax return for gift tax.

4 Amount of gift tax

The tax rate of gift tax is the progressive tax rate, and the applicable tax rate is as follows depending on the taxable value after the basic exemption.

一般贈与財産			特例贈与財産		
基礎控除後の課税価格	一般税率	一般贈与財産に係る控除額	基礎控除後の課税価格	特例税率	特例贈与財産に係る控除額
200 万円以下	10 %	–	200 万円以下	10 %	–
300 万円以下	15 %	10 万円	400 万円以下	15 %	10 万円
400 万円以下	20 %	25 万円	600 万円以下	20 %	30 万円
600 万円以下	30 %	65 万円	1,000 万円以下	30 %	90 万円
1,000 万円以下	40 %	125 万円	1,500 万円以下	40 %	190 万円
1,500 万円以下	45 %	175 万円	3,000 万円以下	45 %	265 万円
3,000 万円以下	50 %	250 万円	4,500 万円以下	50 %	415 万円
3,000 万円超	55 %	400 万円	4,500 万円超	55 %	640 万円

(1) 原則

贈与により財産を取得した者については、基礎控除後の課税価格に上表左の一般贈与財産に係る一般税率を乗じて得た金額から、一般贈与財産に係る控除額を控除して納付すべき贈与税の額を算出します。

(2) 特例

直系尊属から贈与によって財産を取得した者（財産の贈与を受けた年の1月1日において18歳以上の者に限る。ただし、2022年3月31日以前に贈与を受けた場合には、その財産の贈与を受けた年の1月1日において20歳以上の者に限る）については、基礎控除後の課税価格に上表右の特例贈与財産に係る特例税率を乗じて得た金額から、特例贈与財産に係る控除額を控除して納付すべき贈与税の額を算出します。

(3) 外国税額控除

受贈者が在外財産の贈与を受けた場合において、その財産の所在地国において贈与税に相当する税を課されたときは、その課された税に相当する金額を日

General gifted property			Special gifted property		
Taxable value after basic exemption	General tax rate	Deduction for general gifted property	Taxable value after basic exemption	Special tax rate	Deduction for special gifted property
JPY 2 million or less	10%	-	JPY 2 million or less	10%	-
JPY 3 million or less	15%	JPY 100,000	JPY 4 million or less	15%	JPY 100,000
JPY 4 million or less	20%	JPY 250,000	JPY 6 million or less	20%	JPY 300,000
JPY 6 million or less	30%	JPY 650,000	JPY 10 million or less	30%	JPY 900,000
JPY 10 million or less	40%	JPY 1.25 million	JPY 15 million or less	40%	JPY 1.9 million
JPY 15 million or less	45%	JPY 1.75 million	JPY 30 million or less	45%	JPY 2.65 million
JPY 30 million or less	50%	JPY 2.5 million	JPY 45 million or less	50%	JPY 4.15 million
Over JPY 30 million	55%	JPY 4 million	Over JPY 45 million	55%	JPY 6.4 million

(1) Principle

For a person who has acquired properties through gifts, the amount of gift tax to be paid is calculated by deducting the deduction for general gifted properties from the amount obtained by multiplying the taxable value after the basic exemption by the general tax rate for general gifted properties shown on the left side of the above table.

(2) Exception

For a person who has acquired property from a lineal ascendant through gifts (limited to those who are 18 years of age or older as of January 1 of the year in which they received the gifted properties. However, in case of receiving a gift on or before March 31, 2022, it is limited to those who are 20 years of age or older as of January 1 of the year in which they received the gifted properties.), the amount of gift tax to be paid is calculated by deducting the deduction for special gifted properties from the amount obtained by multiplying the taxable value after the basic exemption by the special tax rate for special gifted properties shown on the right side of the above table.

(3) Foreign tax credit

If a donee receives a gift of overseas properties and is subject to a tax equivalent to gift

本の贈与税の額から控除することができます。ただし、日本の贈与税の額を超えて控除することはできません。

tax in the country where the properties are located, the amount equivalent to the tax imposed may be deducted from the amount of gift tax in Japan. However, the deduction cannot exceed the amount of gift tax in Japan.

7 租税条約

1　租税条約の目的

国境を越える経済取引が行われると、納税者の居住地国と進出先国が、同一の所得に対して課税を行うといったことが生じます。こうした二重課税が経済取引の障害とならないように、二つの国の間で課税権の調整を図ったり、主に所得の源泉地国での課税を軽減するような取決めが締結されています。このような国家間の取り決めを「租税条約」といいます。租税条約の目的は、上述した二重課税の排除若しくは低減、脱税の防止、納税者に関する情報の交換や発生した二重課税を可能な限り排除するための措置を取り決めること等です。

2　租税条約の役割

納税者との関係では、租税条約は主に二重課税を排除するために機能します。租税条約では、二重課税排除の対象となる所得を区分しており、事業所得、不動産所得、利子所得、配当所得、使用料所得、譲渡所得、給与所得、その他の所得等のそれぞれについて、課税権の配分、所得源泉地や適用される税率といった事項を定めています。例えば、日本の居住者がA国で利子所得を得た場合に、その利子所得についてA国で課される税の税率は、A国の国内法による税率（例えば20％）ではなく、日本とA国の間の租税条約に定められた税率（例えば10％）に修正されます。租税条約の定めは、条約締結国の国内法の規定に優先して適用されることになりますので、国内法の規定と異なる課税が行われることもよくあります。

7 TAX TREATY

1 Purpose of tax treaty

When cross-border economic transactions are carried out, the country of residence of the taxpayer and the country of destination may impose taxes on the same income. In order to prevent such double taxation from becoming an obstacle to economic transactions, arrangements have been made between the two countries to adjust their taxing rights and to reduce taxes mainly in the source country of income. Such arrangements between countries are called tax treaty. The purpose of a tax treaty is to eliminate or reduce the above-mentioned double taxation, to prevent tax evasion, to exchange information about taxpayers, and to arrange measures to eliminate double taxation that has occurred as far as possible.

2 Role of tax treaty

In the relationship with taxpayers, tax treaties function primarily to eliminate double taxation. The tax treaty classifies income subject to the elimination of double taxation and stipulate the allocation of taxing rights, source country of income, and applicable tax rates for each of the following type of income: business income, real estate income, interest income, dividend income, royalty income, capital gains, employment income, other income, and etc.. For example, if a resident of Japan earns interest income in Country A, the tax rate imposed in Country A on that interest income will be adjusted to the tax rate set forth in the tax treaty between Japan and Country A (e.g., 10%), rather than the rate set by the domestic law of Country A (e.g., 20%). Since the provisions of a tax treaty take precedence over the provisions of the domestic law of the country to which the treaty is concluded, there are many cases where taxation differs from the provisions of the domestic law.

【税務辞典】和英編
Japanese ➡ English

あ

青色事業専従者 blue return business family employee

青色事業専従者給与 salaries paid to blue return business family employee

青色申告書 blue form tax return

青色申告承認申請の却下 rejection of application to filing blue return

青色申告承認の取消し revocation of approval of blue return filing status

青色申告の承認 approval of blue return filing

赤字 deficit, red figure

悪意（法律） bad faith, mala fides

悪意の（法律） in bad faith

預り金 deposits received

頭金 down payment

圧縮記帳 advanced depreciation

圧縮限度額 advanced depreciation limit

後入先出法 last in, first out method (last-in first-out method)

洗替法 reversal method

粗利（益） gross profit

い

以下 or less

閾値 threshold

異議申立て appeal

以降 on or after

遺言 will

遺産 bequest

遺産受取人 legatee

遺産管理人 administrator of bequest

遺産取得税方式 method of taxation on legatee

遺産税方式 method of taxation on bequest

遺産相続 inheritance of bequest

遺産分割 partition of bequest

以上 or more

意匠権 design right

以前 on or before

遺贈 devise

遺贈者 devisor

委託 consignment

委託者 consigner

委託者（信託の） settlor

委託する consign

委託手数料 commission

一時居住者 temporary resident

一時所得 occasional income

一時所得の特別控除額 special deduction for occasional income

著しく低い価額 remarkably low value

一括の lump-sum

一括払いの lump-sum payment

一括比例配分方式 proportional method

一般株式に係る譲渡所得等の金額 capital gain pertaining to unlisted stock

一般株式に係る譲渡損失の金額 capital loss pertaining to unlisted stock

一般管理費 general administrative expenses

一般寄附金 general donation

一般財団法人 general incorporated foundation

一般社団法人 general incorporated association

一般社団法人及び一般財団法人に関する法律 Act on General Incorporated Associations and General Incorporated Foundations

移転価格 transfer price, transfer pricing

移転価格課税 transfer pricing taxation

移転価格事務運営要領 Commissioner's Directive on Operation of Transfer Pricing

移転価格税制 transfer pricing taxation system

移転価格調整 transfer pricing adjustment

移転価格ドキュメンテーション transfer pricing documentation

移転価格の検証 transfer pricing study

移転価格文書 transfer pricing document

移転価格文書化 transfer pricing documentation

移転登記 transfer registration

移動平均 moving average

移動平均法 moving average method

委任（された権限） power

委任状 power of attorney

遺留分 statutory reserved portion

医療費 medical expense

医療費控除 medical expense deduction

印鑑（印影） seal impression

印鑑証明書 certificate of a seal-impression

印紙税 stamp duty

印紙税法 Stamp Tax Act

印章 seal

姻族 relative by affinity

隠蔽 concealment

隠蔽する conceal

う

打切り支給（退職金の） payment of retirement allowance due to termination

請負 contract

請負契約 contract agreement

受付印 reception stamp

受取手形 note receivable

受取配当等の益金不算入 exclusion of dividends received

受取利子 interest income, interest received

受取利息 interest received

裏書 endorsement

裏書人 endorser

裏書譲渡 transfer of endorsed note

売上総利益 gross profit

売上高営業利益率を指標とする取引単位営業利益法 TNMM with operating margin as profit indicator

売上値引 sales discount

売上割戻し sales rebate, rebate on sales

売掛金 account receivable

運送費 transportation cost

運転免許証 driver's license

え

営業外収益 non-operating profit

営業外費用 non-operating expense

営業権 goodwill

営業収入 operating revenue

営業損失 operating loss

営業利益 operating profit

営業利益率　operating margin

永住者　permanent resident

永住者カード（グリーンカード）　green card

永年勤続者の記念品　award in commemoration of the long service of a person

営利法人　profit corporation, for-profit corporation

益金　gross profit (for tax purposes)

益金算入　inclusion

益金算入とする　include

益金不算入　exclusion from gross profit

役務受託者　contract service provider

役務提供　provision of services, service provision

閲覧する（固定資産課税台帳など）　browse

LOB 条項　limitation on benefits provision

延滞金　delinquent charge

延滞した　overdue

延滞している　past due

延滞税　delinquency tax

延滞税の免除　discharge of delinquent tax

延長　extension

延長する　extend

延納　postponement of tax payment

延納（確定申告税額の）　deferred payment of income tax

お

押印　seal

横領　embezzlement

OECD 移転価格ガイドライン　OECD Transfer Pricing Guidelines for Multinational Enterprises and Tax Administrations

OECD 承認アプローチ　Authorized OECD Approach (AOA)

OECD モデル租税条約　OECD Model Tax Convention (on Income and on Capital)

OECD モデル租税条約コメンタリー　commentary on the OECD Model Tax Convention

オープン型投資信託　open-end investment trust

乙欄（源泉徴収税額表の）　column B

覚書　memorandum

親会社　parent company

オンコールサービス　on-call services
解説 特に移転価格税制の文脈で、関連会社が他の関連会社からの問い合わせに即応できる体制を整えている状況を指す。オンコールサービスは関連者間の役務提供とされる。

恩典の享受者（租税条約の）　beneficial owner

か

海外渡航費　overseas travel expense

海外取引　overseas transaction

外貨換算　foreign currency translation

外貨建債権　receivable in foreign currency

外貨建債務　debt in foreign currency

外貨建取引　foreign currency transaction

開業後間もない会社　start-up company

開業費　pre-operating cost, start-up cost, start-up expense

会計監査　accounting audit

会計期間　accounting period

会計基準　accounting standards

会計検査院　Board of Audit

会計原則　accounting principles

会計年度　financial year

外形標準課税　pro-forma taxation, size-based taxation

外国為替及び外国貿易法　Foreign Exchange and Foreign Trade Act

外国為替相場　foreign exchange rate

外国関係会社　controlled foreign corporation [company] (CFC)

外国居住者等所得相互免除法　Mutual Exemption Law for Income of Foreign Resident, etc.

外国源泉税　foreign tax withheld at source, foreign withholding tax

外国口座税務コンプライアンス法　Foreign Account Tax Compliance Act

外国子会社合算税制　CFC rules

外国子会社配当益金不算入制度　foreign dividend exemption system

外国所得税　foreign income tax

外国税額控除　foreign tax credit

外国税額控除方式　credit method

外国駐在員　expatriate

外国転出時所得課税（制度）　exit tax (system)

外国投資信託　foreign investment trust

外国配当　foreign dividend

外国普通法人でなくなった旨の届出書　notification of being no longer a foreign ordinary corporation

外国普通法人となった旨の届出書　notification of becoming a foreign ordinary corporation

外国法人　foreign corporation [company]

介護保険料　medical care insurance premium

解雇予告手当　allowance for dismissal without notice in advance

解散（会社の）　dissolution

解散する（会社が）　dissolve

海事代理士　marine procedure commission agent

会社印　corporation seal

会社分割　spin-off

会社法　Company Act

解除条件　condition subsequent

外為法　Foreign Exchange and Foreign Trade Control Law

外注（加工）費　subcontract cost

回転率　turnover ratio

該当無し　not applicable

開発費　development expense [cost]

買戻し　redemption

買い戻す（自己株式を）　redeem

解約不能のリース　non-cancellable lease

改良費　improvement expense

家屋課税台帳　house tax register book

価格調整　price adjustment

価格調整金　amount for price adjustment

価格調整条項　price adjustment clause

係長（日本の税務当局の役職）　chief

角印 corporation seal

各種所得の金額 amount of income in each class

確定決算において in the accounting procedures by the financial closing

確定した決算に基づき based on the closed accounts

確定申告 annual filing

確定申告が必要な給与所得者 employment income earner required to file final return

確定申告書 annual (tax) return, final tax return

確定税額 final tax

額面株式 par value stock, par value share

額面金額（株式等の） par value, stated value

加工費 processing cost

過誤納 overpayment

過誤納金 overpaid amount

過誤納金の還付 refund of overpaid amount

火災保険 fire insurance

火災保険料 fire insurance premium

加算 addition

加算金 additional charge, additional levy

加算税 additional tax, penalty, penalty tax

貸方 credit

貸方残高 credit balance

家事関連費 expenses related to household

貸倒引当金 allowance for bad debt

貸倒引当金（一般評価金銭債権に係る） general provision for bad debt

過失 negligence

貸付金 loan

貸付金債権 loan receivables

貸付金利子（所法 161 ①十の国内業務関連利子） interest on a loan to those who conduct operation in Japan which is related to that operation

家事費 household expenses

貸家の評価 valuation of rental house

過少課税支払否認ルール undertaxed payments rule

過少資本 thin capitalisation

過少資本税制 thin capitalisation rules

過少申告 underreport

過少申告加算金 additional charge on underreport

過少申告加算税 additional tax on underreport

課す（税金などを） impose, levy

課税 taxation

課税遺産総額 total taxable bequest

課税売上（消費税等） taxable sales

課税売上割合 taxable sales ratio

課税価格 taxable value

課税権 taxing right

課税最低限 tax threshold

課税仕入れ taxable purchase

課税事業者の選択 option to be a taxable business

課税資産と非課税資産の譲渡 transfer of taxable property and non-taxable property

課税主体 sovereign of taxation

課税上透明体 entity transparent for tax purposes, fiscally transparent entity

課税上無視される事業体 disregarded entity

課税所得 taxable profit

課税処分の取消し reversal of taxation

課税総所得金額 total taxable income

課税対象期間 taxable period

課税対象金額 taxable income

課税対象となる事象 taxable event

課税対象取引（消費税等） taxable transaction

課税対象年度 taxable year

課税の繰延べ措置 tax deferral measure

課税の対象となる taxable

課税標準 income tax basis, taxable basis

課税物件 object of taxation

課税文書（印紙税の） taxable document for stamp duty

課税明細書（賦課決定方式における） tax assessment notice

仮装 disguise

仮装経理 disguised accounting

仮装経理に基づく過大申告の場合の更正に伴う法人税額の控除 corporation tax credit due to correction of overpayment based on disguised accounting

仮装する disguise

仮装取引 sham transaction

仮装又は隠蔽 disguise or concealment

過大支払利子税制（と同等の制度） earnings stripping rules

過怠税 delinquency tax

過大な役員給与の損金不算入 exclusion of excess remuneration for director

過大な役員退職給与の損金不算入 exclusion of excess retirement allowance for director

過大納付 overpayment

過大役員報酬 excessive director's compensation [remuneration]

課長（日本の税務当局の役職） director

課徴金 levy

課長補佐（日本の税務当局の役職） deputy director

合併 merger

合併契約書 contract of merger

合併する merge

合併法人 transferee corporation

貸手 lender

角地 corner lot

金型 mould

加入する（年金制度に） enroll

過払いの overpaid

寡夫 widower

寡婦 widow

寡婦控除 exemption for widows

株式 stock, share

株式会社 Kabushiki Kaisha

株式交換 share for share exchange

株式交付費 stock issuance cost

株式償還 share redemption

株式譲渡制限 restriction on share transfer

株式対価 share consideration, stock consideration

株式の消却 retirement of stock

株式の引受け subscription for stock

株式発行 share issuance

株式分割 stock split

株式分配 stock distribution, share distribution

株式併合 reverse stock split, share consolidation, stock consolidation

株式報酬 share-based compensation, stock-based compensation

株式報酬費用 share-based compensation expense, stock-based compensation expense

株主 shareholder

株主資本等変動計算書 statement of changes in shareholders' equity

株主総会 shareholders' meeting

株主総会議事録 minutes of shareholders' meeting

借入金 loan

仮受 VAT output VAT

仮受金 temporary receipts

仮受消費税等 output consumption tax

借方 debit

借方残高 debit balance

仮決算 provisional financial closing

仮差押 provisional seizure

仮執行 provisional execution

仮処分 provisional disposition

借手 borrower

仮登記 provisional registration

仮払金 temporary payments

仮払消費税等 input consumption tax

過料 non-penal fine

為替換算 translation

為替換算差額 translation difference

為替の換算をする translate

為替予約（契約） currency forward contract

簡易課税制度（消費税の） simplified tax system (of consumption tax)

簡易保険 post-office life insurance

換価処分 asset conversion

換価の猶予 grace of asset conversion

関係者 party

監査 audit

監査報告書 audit report

監査法人 auditing corporation

勘定 account

勘定科目内訳明細書 itemised statement of account

勘定科目の一覧表 chart of accounts

関税 customs, customs duties, duties, tariff

関税が課せられる dutiable

関税評価額 customs value

関税率 tariff rate

関税率表 tariff table

間接外国税額控除 indirect foreign tax credit

間接経費 overhead cost, overhead expense

間接税 indirect tax

間接保有（株式等の） indirect shareholding

完全支配関係 100% controlling relationship

還付（税金の） recovery of tax, refund of tax

還付加算金 interest on refund of tax

還付金の益金不算入 exclusion of refund from gross profit

還付金の充当 appropriation of refunded tax

還付する（税金を） refund

還付請求 claim for a tax refund

還付請求権の時効 statute of limitation on refund claim

簡便法 shortcut method

官報 gazette

元本（貸付金等の） principal

管理支配地（基準） place of central management and controll

関連会社 affiliate, affiliate(d) company/affiliate(d) corporation, related company/related corporation, associated company/associated corporation/associated enterprise

関連者 related party

関連者間取引 related party transaction

関連する relevant

き

キープウェル契約 keepwell agreement
解説 主に関連会社間で、例えば親会社が子会社に対して、その子会社がデフォルトを起こすことがないよう資金を供給することを保証する契約。

機械装置 machinery and equipment

機関（社団法人・財団法人の） administrative mechanism

期間が終わる expire

期間損益計算 periodical accounting of profit and loss

企業家 entrepreneur

企業会計原則 financial accounting standards for business enterprise

企業家リスク entreprenueur risk

企業の利得　profits of an enterprise

器具　fixture, equipment

議決権　voting right

危険　risk

期限　term

期限（申告・納税の）　due date, deadline

期限が到来している（申告・納税の）　due

期限後申告　late filing, overdue tax return

期限後の　past due

期限内申告　on-time return

期限内申告書　tax return filed by the due date

期限を過ぎた　overdue

疑似 DES　quasi debt equity swap

期日（申告・納税の）　due date

期首　beginning of accounting period

期首残高　beginning balance, opening balance

期首商品棚卸高　inventory at the beginning of the period

技術役務の提供　technical service provision

基準　standard

基準期間　base period

基準値　threshold

基準年度　base year

机上調査　office audit

机上調査（税務調査の一種）　desk audit

議事録　meeting minutes

規制　regulation

帰属主義　attributable income approach [principle]

帰属所得　imputed income

基礎控除　basic exemption

基礎控除（相続税の）　basic deduction for bequest

既存の　pre-existing

記帳する　carry, post

議定書　protocol

規定する　stipulate

機能事実分析　functional and factual analysis

機能分析　functional analysis

希薄化　dilution

希薄化効果　dilutive effect

揮発油税　Gasoline tax

寄附金　expense of contribution or donation

寄附金課税　taxation on expense of contribution or donation

寄附金控除　deduction for contributions or donations

寄附金の損金算入限度額　deductible limit of donation expense for tax purposes

寄附行為　endowment

寄附する　donate

基本的利益　routine profit

期末　end of accounting period

期末残高　ending balance, closing balance

期末商品棚卸高　inventory at the end of the period

キャッシュボックス　cash box　解説 重要な機能を果たすことなく多額の資金を運用し、あるいは保有する無形資産からの収益をプールしている会社。日本の外国子会社合算税制ではペーパーカンパニーとしての合算課税を受ける。

吸引力　force of attraction

旧株　old stock

究極の親会社　ultimate parent company

旧個人年金保険料　old personal pension insurance premium

求償権　right of indemnity

旧生命保険料　old life insurance premium

旧長期損害保険料　former long-term casualty insurance premiums

休眠会社　shell company

休眠の　dormant

給与支払事務所　salary-paying office

給与支払事務所等の移転（廃止）届出書 Notification of Relocation (Closure) of a Salary-Paying Office

給与支払報告書 salary payment record, salary (payment) slip, payslip

給与支払事務所等の移転届出書 Notification of Relocation of a Salary-Paying Office

給与支払事務所等の開設届出書 Notification of Establishment of a Salary-Paying Office

給与所得 employment income, salary income

給与所得・退職所得等の所得税徴収高計算書 Statement (tax payment slip) of Income Tax Collected from Employment/Retirement Income, etc. (for General Purposes and the Special Provision for Due Dates)

給与所得者 employment income earner, earner of salary

給与所得者の（特定増改築等）住宅借入金等特別控除 special credit for loans, etc. related to a dwelling (specific additions or improvements, etc.)

給与所得者の（特定増改築等）住宅借入金等特別控除申告書 Application for Special Credit for Loans, etc. Related to a Dwelling (Specific Additions or Improvements, etc.) for Employment Income Earner

給与所得者の扶養控除等（異動）申告書 Application for (change in) Exemption for Dependents of employment Income Earner

給与所得者の保険料控除申告書 Application for Deduction for Insurance Premiums for Employment Income Earner

給与所得とみなされる経済的利益 economic benefit regarded as salary income

給与所得の源泉徴収税額表（月額表/日額表） withholding tax amount table for employment income (monthly table/daily table)

給与所得の源泉徴収票 employment income withholding record

給与テーブル payroll table

給与明細 pay stub, pay slip, salary (payment) slip, payslip

教育訓練費 staff training expense

教育資金 educational funds

教育資金の一括贈与 lump-sum donation of educational funds

行政救済 administrative remedy

行政権 administrative power

行政行為 administrative action

行政裁量 administrative discretion

行政事件訴訟法 Administrative Case Litigation Act

強制執行 compulsory execution

行政指導 administrative direction, administrative guidance

行政処分 administrative disposition, administrative disposition

行政訴訟 administrative litigation

強制調査 compulsory tax investigation

行政通達 administrative circular

行政手続法 Administrative Procedure Act

行政不服審査法 Administrative Complaint Review Act

行政法 administrative law

業績連動給与 performance-based compensation

兄弟会社 sister company

供託金 deposited money, money paid into court

供託所 deposit office

供託する deposit

供託する（金銭を） pay money into court

供託物 deposited article

供託法 Deposit Act

共通報告基準 Common Reporting Standard (CRS)

協同組合 cooperative association

業務委託契約書 letter of engagement

協約 convention

許可 grant, permission

居住者 resident

居住者証明 certificate of residence

居住者証明書　residency certificate

居住制限納税義務者　resident taxpayer with limitation

居住地　domicile

居住地国　country of residence [domicile]

居住地振り分けルール　tie(-)breaker rule

居住無制限納税義務者　resident taxpayer without limitation

居住用財産　residential property

拠出（社会保険などに対する）　contribution

拠出する　contribute

居所　residence

銀行印　bank seal

均等償却　straight line method

均等割（住民税）　per capita levy, per capita tax

禁反言の法理　principle of estoppel

勤労学生　working student

勤労学生控除　exemption for working students

く

偶発債務　contingent liability

国等に対する寄附金　donation to government, etc.

国別報告事項　Country by Country Report (CbCR)

区分経理　sectional accounting

区分所有権　sectional ownership

組合　partnership

組合の持分　partnership interest

繰越し　carried forward

繰越控除限度超過額　unused foreign tax

繰越欠損金　tax losses brought forward, losses carried forward, net loss carryforward

繰越欠損金（税務上）　tax loss carried forward

繰越控除　carry-over deduction

繰越控除余裕額　unused credit limit

繰延資産　deferred expense

繰戻し　carry back

グループ会社間の　intercompany

グループ間役務提供　inter-group services

グループ法人税制　enterprise group taxation system, group taxation regime

黒字　black in figure, positive balance, surplus

グロスアップ　gross up　**解説** 給与、報酬、使用料等の支払を受ける者が税引前の金額で受け取ることができるように源泉税の金額分を本来の報酬の総額（グロス）に上乗せ（アップ）すること。（本来の報酬金額＋グロスアップ額）－源泉税額＝本来の報酬金額という算式であらわすことができる。

グロスアップ計算　gross up computation

け

経営指導念書　keepwell letter

経営指導料　management fee

経営判断原則　business judgement rule

軽課税国［地域］　low tax jurisdiction

経過措置　transitional measure

経過措置規定　transitional provision

軽減　relief

軽減する　relieve

軽減税率　reduced tax rate

軽減税率適用法人（法人事業税等の）　corporation entitled to reduced tax rate

軽減税率不適用法人（法人事業税等の） corporation unentitled to reduced tax rate

経済協力開発機構 Organisation of Economy and Commercial Development (OECD)

経済産業省 Ministry of Economy, Trade and Industry

経済的観察法 interpretation based on economic realty

経済的実質 economic substance

経済的二重課税 economic double taxation

経済的利益 economic benefit, fringe benefit

経済的利益（金銭以外の） benefit in kind

計算 calculation, computation

計算書類 accounting documents

計算する calculate, compute

経常損失 ordinary loss

経常利益 ordinary profit

継続して１年以上居所を有する者（個人） person continuously having a residence in Japan for one year or more

継続性の原則 principle of consistency

係属中の訴訟事案 pending case, pending lawsuit

競売 auction

経費補助金 compensation for expense and loss

契約 agreement, arrangement, contract

契約者配当 policyholder dividends

契約書 contract, engagement letter

契約上の contractual

消印 date stamp

決議 resolution

決議の日 resolution date

決算（会計の） financial closing

決算日 closing date

決算日レート（為替換算のための） closing rate

月次の monthly

欠損金 net loss, net operating loss

欠損金（税務上） tax loss

欠損金の繰越し tax loss carryforward

欠損金の繰戻還付 net loss carry back

欠損金の繰戻し tax loss carryback

決定（税務当局による処分としての） determination

気配相場のある株式の評価 valuation of over-the-counter stock

原価基準法 cost plus method

原価計算 cost accounting

原価差額 cost variance

減価償却期間（有形減価償却資産以外） amortisation period

減価償却期間（有形固定資産） depreciation period

減価償却限度額（有形減価償却資産以外） deductible limit of amortisation amount

減価償却限度額（有形減価償却資産） deductible limit of depreciation amount

減価償却資産 depreciable asset

減価償却超過額 excessive depreciation expenses

減価償却費 capital allowance

減価償却不足額 short depreciation

減価償却方法（有形減価償却資産以外） amortisation method

減価償却方法（有形減価償却資産） depreciation method

減価償却率 depreciation rate

減価償却累計額 accumulated depreciation

研究開発税制 tax system for research and development

現金 cash

現金主義 cash basis

現金出納帳 cash book

権限 competence

権限のある competent

権限のある当局 competent authority

健康診断 medical check-up

健康保険 health (care) insurance

健康保険（従業員等の） Employee' Health Insurance

減算 subtraction

減算する subtract

減資 reduction in capital, share redemption, stock redemption

検収 inspection

検収基準 customer acceptance basis

検証対象法人 tested company

源泉所得税 income tax withheld at source, withholding income tax

源泉所得税及び復興特別所得税の誤納額還付請求書 application for refund of erroneously paid withholding income tax and special income tax for reconstruction

源泉所得税の納期の特例 special provision for due dates for withholding income tax

源泉所得税の納期の特例の承認に関する申請書 Application for Approval Made in Relation to the Special Provision for Due Dates for Withholding Income Tax

源泉税 withholding tax

源泉徴収義務 obligation to withhold tax, withholding obligation

源泉徴収義務者 withholding agent

源泉徴収税額表 withholding tax amount table

源泉徴収票 withholding record

源泉徴収免除証明書 certificate of exemption from withholding

源泉分離課税 separate withholding taxation at source

源泉分離課税の対象となる所得 income subject to separate withholding taxation at source

県庁（行政機関） prefectural government

県庁（の建物） prefectural office

限定承認 qualified acceptance of inheritance

限度 limit, limitation

現物給付 benefits in kind, payment in kind

現物給与 benefits in kind, payment in kind, salary in kind

現物出資 contribution in kind

現物相場 spot exchange rate

現物対価 consideration in kind

現物取引 spot transaction

現物配当 dividend in kind

現物分配 distribution in kind

現物報酬 consideration in kind

憲法 constitution

憲法（上）の constitutional

現務の結了 conclusion of current business

権利金 key money, premium

権利証 muniment of title

権利証書 deed

こ

後 after

公益財団法人 public interest incorporated foundation

公益社団法人 public interest incorporated association

公益社団法人等寄附金特別控除 special credit for contributions to public interest incorporated associations, etc.

公益法人 corporation in the public interest

公課 public charges

公開会社 public company

高価買入資産 asset purchased at an unreasonably high value

豪華社宅 luxury residence

交換公文（租税条約を含む条約の） exchange of note (E/N)

交換差益 capital gain on exchange of properties

恒久的施設 permanent establishment (PE)

恒久的施設帰属所得 profit attributable to permanent establishment

工業所有権 industrial property right

工具 tools

口座 account

交際費 entertainment expense [cost], social expenses

公示 public notification

工事完成基準 completed construction method

工事進行基準 percentage of completion method

工事負担金 payment by beneficiary

控除（特に個人所得税における） allowance

控除限度超過額（外国税額控除制度の） excess foreign tax

控除すべき公租公課 taxes and other public charges to be deducted

控除すべき債務 liabilities to be deducted

控除する（所得から） deduct

控除対象外国法人税（の額） creditable foreign tax

控除対象配偶者 spouses covered by exemption

控除対象扶養親族 dependents covered by an exemption

控除できる（所得から） deductible

控除余裕額（外国税額控除制度の） excess credit limit

更新（契約などの） renewal

更新料 renewal fee [charge]

更正 correction, reassessment

構成員課税 pass-through taxation 解説 パススルー事業体の構成員に直接税を課すこと。

構成員課税 flow-through taxation 解説 フロースルー（＝パススルー）事業体の構成員に直接税を課すこと。

構成企業 constituent entity

更正処分 tax reassessment

更正する correct, reassess

構成する constituent

更正通知書 correction notice, notice of correction, reassessment notice, tax reassessment notice

厚生年金 welfare pension

厚生年金保険（従業員の） Employee’ Pension Insurance

構造 structure

後続の subsequent 例 subsequent fiscal year（後続の事業年度）

構築物 structure

公定歩合 official discount rate

公定力 tentative validity

公的年金 public pension

公的年金等 public pension, etc.

香典 Koden (cash offering for a funeral)

合同運用信託 joint trust

合同会社 Goudou Kaisha

公認会計士 certified public accountant (CPA)

公売 public auction

公布 promulgation

合法的な legal

甲欄（源泉徴収税額表の） column A

超える more than

コーポレートインバージョン corporate inversion

国外関連者 foreign related company/foreign affiliate(d) company

国外関連者に対する寄附金 donation to foreign affiliate(s)

国外関連取引 controlled transaction, related party transaction

国外源泉所得 foreign source(d) income

国外財産調書 reporting form for assets located outside Japan

国外所得免除方式 exemption method cf. tax credit method, territorial tax, territorial tax(action) system

国外取引（消費税法の） foreign transaction

国債 government bonds

国際課税 international tax [taxation]

国際観光旅客税 International Tourist Tax

国際的二重課税 international double taxation

国際連盟（国連） United Nations

国税 national tax

国税局 Regional Taxation Bureau

国税局長（日本の税務当局の役職） regional commissioner

国税査察官 tax inspectator

国税査察官（日本の国税局の役職） investigator

国税庁 National Tax Agency

国税調査官（日本の税務当局の役職） examiner

国税徴収法 National Taxes Collection Act [Law]

国税徴収法施行規則 Regulation for Enforcement of the National Tax Collection Act

国税徴収法施行令 Order for Enforcement of the National Tax Collection Act

国税庁長官 Commissioner of the National Tax Agency (of Japan)

国税通則法 Act [Law] on General Rules for National Taxes

国税通則法施行規則 Regulation for Enforcement of the General Rules for National Taxes Act

国税通則法施行令 Order for General Rules for National Taxes Act

国税不服審判所 National Tax Tribunal

国籍 nationality, citizenship

国内源泉所得 domestic source income

国内取引（消費税法の） domestic transaction

国内にある土地等の譲渡による対価 consideration for the transfer of land, etc. located in Japan

国内において業務を行う者から受ける当該業務に係る使用料［貸付金の利子］ royalty [loan interest] received from a person pertaining to domestic operations conducted by that person in Japan

国内法 domestic law

国内法による二重課税の軽減制度 unilateral relief

国民健康保険 National Health Insurance

国民健康保険税 national health insurance tax

国連モデル租税条約 United Nations Model Double Taxation Convention between Developed and Developing Countries

個人事業主 sole proprietorship

個人事業の開業届出書 Notification of Establishment, etc. of Sole Proprietorship

個人住民税 individual inhabitant tax

個人所得税 individual income tax, personal income tax

個人所得税の申告書 individual income tax return, personal income tax return

個人年金保険料 personal pension insurance premium

個人の事業税 individual business tax

個人番号 individual number

個人番号カード individual number card

個人番号通知書 notification card of individual number

コストプラス（契約） cost plus agreement [contract]

戸籍 family register

戸籍謄本 copy of family register

国境税調整 border tax adjustment

国庫補助金 government grant [subsidy]

固定資産課税台帳 fixed assets tax ledger

固定資産税 fixed asset(s) tax, property tax

固定資産税の減額 reduction of fixed assets tax

固定資産税の免除 exemption of fixed assets tax

固定資産台帳 fixed asset register

固定的な事業の場所 fixed place of business

固定費 fixed cost

固定負債 non-current liability

誤謬修正（過去年度の会計数値の） correction of prior period errors

個別対応方式 itemised deduction

個別評価金銭債権に対する貸倒引当金 bad debt provision for specifically evaluated receivables

個別法（棚卸資産の評価方法） specific identification method

コミッショネア commissionaire 解説 わが国商法の問屋（といや）に相当する事業形態。自らが売買契約の当事者となって他人の商品等を販売する。コミッショネアは当該他人から手数料を受領できる。巨大企業が多量の製品をコミッショネアを通じて販売した場合に、市場国においてコミッショネアの手数料しか所得が生じないことが国際課税で長く問題視されてきた。

顧問（会社の役職） counselor

雇用促進税制 tax system for job creation

ゴルフ会員権 golf club membership

ゴルフクラブの入会金 membership fee for golf club

ゴルフ場利用税 golf course use tax

根拠証憑 supporting evidence

根拠資料 supporting material

コンプライアンス業務 tax compliance 解説 税務・会計の文脈において、特に企業の記帳及び申告納税業務をこのように称することがある

さ

サービス PE service PE 解説 役務提供地国に物理的な恒久的施設が存在しない場合でも、その国で役務提供（サービス）活動を行ったことをもって恒久的施設があるものとみなされるときのその役務提供活動をいう。役務提供地国は、サービス PE を根拠として役務提供の対価に対して源泉地課税を行う。通常は一定期間以上の継続的活動が要件とされている。

サービス受託 contract service

災害 casualty

災害被害者に対する租税の減免、徴収猶予等に関する法律 Act on Exemption, Reduction or Postponement of Collection of Taxes for Disaster Victims

裁決 decision

裁決（国税不服審判所の） decision (made by the National Tax Tribunal)

債権 claim

債権の取立て collection of claim

在庫 stock

最高裁判所 Supreme Court

財産 property

財産債務明細書 statement of assets and liabilities

財産状況の調査（会社の清算における） property status survey

財産の換価 cash conversion of property

財産の所在 location of property

財産分与 distribution of property

財産目録（清算会社の） inventory of property

最終仕入原価法 last purchase price method

再調査請求 request for reexamination

再調査の請求 request for re-examination

最低基準 minimum standard, de minimis

裁判 trial

裁判所 tribunal

裁判の judicial

再販売価格 resale price

再販売価格基準法 resale price method

債務控除 deduction of liabilities [debts]

財務省 Ministry of Finance

財務省関税局 Customs and Tariff Bureau, Ministry of Finance

財務省主税局 tax bureau, Ministry of Finance

財務省令 Ministry of Finance Ordinance

債務の弁済 discharge of the obligation

債務不履行 default

債務免除 discharge of indebtedness

在留資格 status of residence

裁量 discretion

裁量信託 discretionary trust

先物レート（為替） forward rate

作成（書類の） preparation

作成する（書類を） prepare

差押 seizure, attachment

差押禁止財産 property prohibited from seizure

差押の解除 release of seizure

差押の猶予 suspension of seizure

雑収入 miscellaneous income

雑所得 miscellaneous income

雑損控除 casualty loss deduction

雑損失 miscellaneous loss

雑多な miscellaneous

雑費 miscellaneous expense

残業 overtime

残業手当 overtime allowance

三親等内の姻族 any person within third degree of relationship by affinity

残存耐用年数 remaining useful life

残余財産 residual property

残余財産の分配 distribution of residual property

残余利益分割法 residual profit split method

山林所得 timber income

し

シークレット・コンパラブル secret comparable 解説 移転価格税制において、税務当局が質問検査権を行使して入手する、同業他社が行う第三者間取引における価格情報をいう。

仕入税額控除 purchase tax credit

死因贈与 donetion due to death

仕掛品 goods in process

自家消費 self-consumption

敷金 caution money, key money, lease deposit, security deposit

直物レート spot (exchange) rate

事業概況説明書 summary statement of business

事業者向け電気通信利用役務の提供 B2B services provided via electronic and telecommunication networks

事業所税 business office tax

事業税 business tax, enterprise tax

事業専従者 white return business family employee

事業専従者控除 deduction of salaries paid to white return business family employee

事業体 entity

事業的規模（不動産所得の） business scale

事業主 proprietor

事業年度 business year, financial year, fiscal year

事業の管理の場所 place of management

事業用資産の買換え replacement of business property

試験研究費 research and development expense

試験研究費に係る税額控除 tax credit for research and development expense

施行（法令の） enforcement

施行規則 regulation for enforcement

時効の中断 interruption of statute of limitations

時効の停止 suspension of statute of limitations

施行日 date of enforcement

施行令 order for enforcement

自己株式 own share, treasury share, treasury stock

自己株式の購入 share repurchase, stock buyback

自己株式の取得（買い戻し） redemption of treasury stock

自己株式の消却 retirement of treasury shares

自己株式の処分 disposal of treasury stocks

事後の ex post

自己否認 voluntary adjustment

資産計上 capitalization

資産性所得 passive income

資産の評価 valuation of assets

資産の評価益の益金不算入 exclusion from income of profit from valuation of asset

資産の評価損の損金不算入 exclusion from deductible expense of loss from valuation of asset

事実婚 de facto marital relationship

事実上婚姻関係と同様の事情にあると認められる者 person who is conceived to be in a de facto marital relationship

事実分析 factual analysis

自署 signature

地震保険料 earthquake insurance premium

地震保険料控除　deduction for earthquake insurance premium

事前確定届出給与　director's fixed compensation notified in advance

事前確認申請　advance price arrangement, advance price agreement（主に米国）

事前照会制度　advance ruling

自然人　natural person

慈善信託　charitable trust

事前相談　pre-filing consultation

事前通知　advance notification of audit

事前の　ex ante

市町村の　municipal

市町村民税（住民税の一部）　municipal (inhabitant) tax

実印　registered seal

実現主義　realisation principle

実現する（リスクなどが）　materialise

執行（行政行為の）　enforcement

実行関税率表　tariff schedule

実効税率　effective tax rate

失効日　expiration date

執行役員　executive officer

実査　physical inspection

実質（所得者）課税の原則　principle of taxation on beneficial owner

実質主義　substance over form doctrine

実質的な　substantial

実質的に　substantially

実地棚卸　physical inventory count

実地調査　field audit

失敗した　failure to

質問検査権　authority to inquire and inspect

質問書　questionnaire

実用新案権　utility model patent

支店利益税　branch profits tax

自動車重量税　motor vehicle tonnage tax

自動車取得税　automobile acquisition tax

自動車税　automobile tax, motor vehicle tax

自動的情報交換　Automatic Exchange of Information (AEOI)

使途不明金　expenditure unaccounted for

支配関係　controlling relationship

支配される　controlled

支配している　controlling

支配する　control

支払義務の消滅（例えば源泉徴収のタイミングとして）　extinguish of payment obligation

支払賃借料　rental expense

支払通知書（還付金の）　note of payment

支払利子　interest paid

支払調書　payment record

四分位　quartile

四分位値の範囲内　interquartile

四分位幅　interquartile range

四分位分析　quartile analysis

司法権　judicial power

司法権（の及ぶ範囲）　jurisdiction

司法上の　judicial, juridical

司法書士　judicial scrivener

資本（等）取引　capital transaction

資本関係図　capital structure diagram, chart of shareholders, group organisation chart

資本金　capital, issued capital, issued share capital, stated capital

資本金（払込資本）　paid-in capital

資本準備金　capital reserve, legal capital reserve

資本剰余金　capital surplus

資本的支出　capital expenditure, capital expense

資本の払戻し　repayment of capital

資本割（事業税の）　capital levy

社員（社団法人・財団法人の）　member

社会保険　social insurance

社会保険税 social insurance tax

社会保険制度 social insurance system

社会保険料 contribution to social security, social insurance premium

社会保険料一括払戻し lump-sum withdrawal payment

社会保険料控除 deduction for social insurance premiums

社会保険労務士 social insurance labor consultant

社会保障協定 social security agreement

社外流出 drain

市役所 city government, city office, municipal office

市役所（建物としての） city hall

借地権 leasehold (right)

社債 corporate bonds, debenture

社債発行費 bond issuance expense [cost]

社宅 company residence

収益 revenue

収益事業 profit-making business

収益的支出 revenue expense

収益認識 revenue recognition

収益の認識基準 revenue recognising standard

収益保証金 compensation for revenue

重加算金 heavy additional charge

重加算税 heavy additional tax, heavy penalty tax

重過失 gross negligence

従業員持株制度 employee stock ownership plan (ESOP)

就業規則 rules of employment

住所（税務上の） domicile

自由職業者条項 article on independent personal services

住所を有する者（個人） a person having a domicile in Japan

州税 state (income) tax（米国等）

修正申告 amendment

修正申告書 amended (tax) return

自由選択の optional

修繕費 repair expense [cost]

従属代理人 dependent agent

住宅取得資金に係る借入金の年末残高等証明書 Certificate for Year End Balance of Loan for Acquisition of Dwelling

住宅手当 housing allowance

住宅ローン控除 special credit for loans, etc. related to a dwelling (specific additions or improvements, etc.)

従たる給与 salary from secondary source

充当 appropriation

収入印紙 revenue stamp

十分である suffice

十分な sufficient

住民税 inhabitant tax

住民票 certificate of residence

収用 expropriation

収用する expropriate

重要な significant, substantial

終了（有効期限などの） expiration

16 歳未満の扶養親族 dependent(s) under sixteen years old

受益者（信託の） beneficiary

受益者等課税信託 trust of which beneficiary, etc. is subject to tax

授権資本 registered capital

酒税 liquor tax

酒税法 Liquor Tax Act

受贈益 gift profit

受贈者 donee

受託者 entrustee

受託者（委託業務の） consignee

受託者（信託における） trustee, fiduciary（trustee より広い概念）

受託製造業者　contract manufacturer

出荷　shipping

出荷基準　shipping basis, shipping standard

出向　secondment

出向契約　secondment agreement

出向先法人　host company

出向させる　second

出向者　seconded employee [personnel], secondee

出向元法人　home company

出国　emigration

出国税　departure tax, exit tax

出資　capital contribution, contribution

出資する　contribute

出訴期間　limitation of actions

受動（的）所得　passive income

取得価額　acquisition cost

取得原価　historical cost

取得時換算法　method of translation at historical rate

取得費　acquistion cost

主任（日本の税務当局の役職）　assistant chief

受忍義務（税務調査における納税者の）　obligation not to interfere

守秘義務　confidentiality (obligation)

主要目的テスト　principal purpose test

受領　receipt

種類　class

種類株式　class shares

準確定申告　quasi final return

準角地　quasi corner lot

純資産価額方式　net asset method

純支払利子　net interest payment

純支払賃料　net rent payment

純損失　net loss

純損失の繰戻し　carryback of net loss

準備的活動　preparatory activity

条　article

障害者　person(s) with disabilities

障害者控除　exemption for persons with disabilities

奨学金　scholarships

少額減価償却資産　small sum depreciable asset

償還　redemption

償還する　redeem

小規模企業共済等掛金控除　deduction of small-scale enterprise mutual aid premiums, etc.

小規模事業者　small-scale enterprise

消却　cancellation, retirement

償却限度額　maximum amount of depreciation

償却資産税　depreciable assets tax

承継　succession

承継人　successor

承継法人　successor

使用権　right of use

使用収益の権利　usufruct

譲受人　transferee

上場株式　listed stock

上場株式に係る譲渡所得等の金額　capital gain pertaining to listed stock

上場株式に係る譲渡損失の金額　capital loss pertaining to listed stock

上場企業　listed company

上席国税調査官（日本の税務当局の役職）　senior examiner

使用貸借　loan for use

譲渡　alienation, transfer

譲渡（する）　alienate, transfer

譲渡制限付株式　restricted stock

譲渡担保　mortgage

譲渡人　transferor

譲渡費用　transfer cost

譲渡利益　capital gain

使用人兼務役員　employee-director

消費税　consumption tax

消費税及び地方消費税　consumption tax and local consumption tax

消費税の申告書　consumption tax return

消費税法　Consumption Tax Act

消費税法施行規則　Regulation for Enforcement of the Consumption Tax Act

消費税法施行令　Order for Enforcement of the Consumption Tax Act

消費貸借　loan for consumption

商標権　trademark right

情報申告　information return

証明書　certificate

消滅会社（合併による）　merged company

条約　convention, treaty

条約漁り　treaty shopping 解説 →「トリーティショッピング」を参照

剰余金　surplus

賞与に対する源泉徴収税額の算出率の表　table for calculating withholding amount for bonuses

賞与引当金　allowance for bonus

使用料　royalty

省令　regulation for encforcement

条例　ordinance

省令（具体的な省令ではなく一般的に省令というとき）　ministerial regulation

条例（市町村の）　municipal ordinance

条例（都道府県の）　prefectural ordinance

除外する（益金から）　exclude

書画骨とう品　painting and antique

所轄税務署長　district director of the competent tax office

除却（固定資産の）　retirement

職業専門家が払うべき正当な注意　due professional care

職務分掌　segregation of duties

職務分掌規程　rules on segregation of duties

所在地　situs

所得（に対する）税　income tax

所得拡大促進税制　tax system for salary growth

所得合算ルール　income inclusion rule

所得源泉　source of income

所得税及び復興特別所得税の予定納税額の減額申請書　Application Form for Reduction of Estimated Income Tax and Restoration Special Income Tax Prepayment

所得税額控除　income tax credit

所得税徴収高計算書　Statement of Collected Income Tax

所得税法（日本の）　Income Tax Act [Law] (of Japan)

所得税法施行規則　Regulation for Enforcement of the Income Tax Act

所得税法施行令　Order for Enforcement of the Income Tax Act

所得割　per income levy

処分（行政）　disposition

処分益　gain on disposal of ～

処分行政庁　disposition authority

署名　autograph

所有権　ownership, title

所有権移転外ファイナンスリース　finance lease without transfer of ownership, non-ownership-transfer finance lease

所有権移転ファイナンスリース　finance lease with transfer of ownership, ownership-transfer finance lease

自力執行権（税務官庁の）　self-enforcement

資料　material

白色申告　white return

仕訳（日記）帳　journal

仕訳（の入力）　journal entry

仕訳伝票　journal slip

人員　personnel

人格のない社団等 association or foundation without juridical personality

新株発行費 share-issuing expense

信義誠実の原則 principle of good faith

申告 declaration

申告期限の延長 extension of tax (return) filing deadline, extension of time to file tax return

申告所得税 self-assessed income tax

申告書の作成 tax return preparation

申告する declare

申告調整 adjustment of final return

申告調整する make adjustment of final return

申告納税 self assessment

申告納税方式 self assessment system

申告分離課税 separate self-assessment taxation

新個人年金保険料 new personal pension insurance premium

審査請求 request for reconsideration

真実性の原則 principle of truth

信書で by correspondence delivery

申請（税務上の） application

申請書 application form

新生命保険料 new life insurance premium

親族 relative

親族関係書類 documents concerning relatives

身体障害者手帳 physical disability certificate

信託 trust

信託財産 trust estate

信託財産責任負担債務 obligation to be performed with property belonging to trust estate

信託財産に係る資産及び負債 asset and liability belonging to trust estate

信託受益権 beneficial interest in trust

信託証書 trust deed

信託利益 profit from trust

進捗度（工事進行基準における） stage of completion of contracted activity

人的役務 personal service

人的役務の提供 provision of personal service

人的役務の提供事業 business providing personal service

人的役務の提供事業の対価 consideration received by a corporation [an individual] that conducts a business where that corporation [individual] provides personal resources rendering specific professional services

人的控除 personal exemption

審判所 tribunal

信用状 letter of credit

し す せ

す

推計 estimate

推計課税 presumptive assessment, taxation by estimate

スイッチ OTC 医薬品 switch OTC drugs

スーパーロイヤルティ条項 super royalty provision 解説 米国の移転価格制度において、無形資産の譲渡対価を税務当局が事後的に修正することを認める規定。

ストックオプション stock option

せ

税（金） tax

税（法）の見地からすると for tax purpose(s)

税額 tax amount

税額控除 tax credit

税額控除する credit

税額の算定（賦課課税方式の税目に関して税務当局が行うもの） assessment

税関 customs

正規の簿記の原則 principle of orderly system of bookkeeping

税金 levy

税金が課されない tax free

税金の還付 tax refund

税金の計算 tax calculation, tax computation

税金の申告 tax filing

税金を納付すべき義務 tax liability

生計費 cost of living

税源浸食及び利益の移転 Base Erosion and Profit Shifting (BEPS)

税源浸食への対抗措置 Global Anti-Base Erosion Proposal

制限する limit

制限無く indefinitely

税込み（で、の） including tax, tax inclusive, with tax

清算 settlement, winding up

清算（会社の） liquidation

清算結了 completion of liquidation

清算事務 administration of the settlement [liquidation]

清算する settle

清算する（会社を） liquidate, settle

清算中の法人 liquidating corporation

清算手続 settlement procedures

清算人 liquidator

清算人会 board of liquidators

清算配当 liquidation dividend [distribution]

精算表 worksheet

清算費用 liquidation cost, settlement fee

精神障害者保健福祉手帳 mental disability certificate

税制 tax regime, tax system

税制改正 tax reform

税制改正法案 tax reform bill

税制上の優遇措置 tax concession, tax incentive

税制適格ストックオプション tax-qualified stock option

税制適格の qualified, tax-qualified

税制適格要件 qualifying conditions for tax purposes

税制非適格ストックオプション non-qualified stock option

税制非適格の non tax-qualified

生前贈与 gift during life

製造請負 contract manufacturing

製造原価 manufacturing cost

政党等寄附金特別控除 special credit for contributions to political parties

税に関する情報交換協定 tax information exchange agreement

税に関する法令の遵守 tax compliance

税抜き（で、の） excluding tax, tax exclusive, without tax

税引き後 after tax, net of (income) tax, post tax

税法 tax code, tax law, tax legislation

税法に定める期間計算の特例 special rule for count of period stipulated in the tax code

税務署 tax office

税務上の for tax purpose(s)

税務上の管轄地域 tax jurisdiction

税務上の繰越欠損金の合計 accumulated tax losses, cumulative tax losses

税務署長（日本の税務当局の役職） district director

税務申告 tax declaration

税務申告書 tax return

税務申告等の税に関する法令遵守のための業務 tax compliance service

税務相談 tax consultation

税務訴訟 tax case

税務代理 tax proxy

税務代理権限証書 power of attorney for tax affairs

税務調査 investigation, tax audit, tax examination

税務調査官 tax auditor, tax examiner

税務調査未済の open

税務調整 adjustment for taxable income

税務当局 tax authorities

税務の申告書 tax form

生命保険 life insurance

生命保険契約等に基づく年金 pension based on a life insurance contract, etc.

生命保険契約に関する権利 right pertaining to life insurance contract

生命保険料 life insurance premium

生命保険料控除 deduction for life insurance premiums

税理士 certified tax accountant

税率 tax rate

政令 cabinet order, order for enforcement

セービング条項 saving clause 解説 租税条約の条項が、原則として条約締約国のその居住者に対する課税を妨げないという考え方。

セーフハーバールール safe harbour rule 解説 税務当局によって示される、税法の解釈や適用に係る基準。取引に係る料率や利益率などが税務上適正なものとして取り扱われる限度を示されることが多い。

セールアンドリースバック sale and lease back transaction 解説 資産の所有者がその資産を売却した後に賃借する取引形態をいう。資産の売却によって一時的に資金が流入する財務（借入れ）効果、セールアンドリースバック取引がオペレーティングリースに該当する場合には、その資産はリースを受ける会社においてオフバランスとなることによって総資産の額が減少するといった効果があるとされる。

セグメント損益 segmented profit or loss 解説 移転価格税制において、取引単位で営業利益率を算定する必要がある場合に、その取引単位ごとに区分して算定される営業損益をいう。

世帯主 head of the household

積極財産 positive assets

節税 tax saving

セルフメディケーション税制 self-medication tax system

善意（法律） bona fides, good faith

善意の（法律） in good faith

善管注意義務 duty of due care of prudent manager, prudent man rule

宣言規定 declaratory stipulation

全世界所得 worldwide income

全世界所得課税方式 worldwide system

選択（できること） option

前年 previous year

占有 occupation

占有する occupy

そ

総額主義 gross amount principle

総括主査（日本の国税局の役職） deputy chief examiner

総括上席国税調査官（日本の税務当局の役職） deputy chief examiner

総勘定元帳 general ledger

創業記念品等 gift commemorating startups, etc.

送金関係書類 documents concerning remittances

総合課税 comprehensive income taxation

総合主義 entire income approach [principle]

相互協議 mutual agreement procedure

相互主義 reciprocity

相互主義の reciprocal

相殺 offset

葬式費用 funeral expenses

相次相続 successive inheritance

相次相続控除 deduction for successive inheritance

総収入 gross income

総所得金額 total net income

相続 inheritance

相続時精算課税 settlement of inheritance tax at succession

相続税 estate tax, inheritance tax

相続税法 Inheritance Tax Act [Law]

相続税法施行規則 Regulation for Enforcement of the Inheritance Tax Act

相続税法施行令 Order for Enforcement of the Inheritance Tax Act

相続人 heir

相続放棄 waiving of inheritance

相続を放棄した者 person who renounced inheritance

送達 service

相談役 advisor

相当の地代 reasonable rent fee

総費用 full cost

総費用営業利益率 ratio of operating profit to total cost

総費用営業利益率を利益指標とする取引単位営業利益法 cost-based TNMM, TNMM with ratio of operating profit to total cost

総平均法 gross average method

双方居住者振り分け規定 tiebreaker rule

贈与 donation, gift

贈与契約 donation contract

贈与税 gift tax

創立費 organisation cost

ソースルール source rule **解説** どのような所得を国内源泉所得とするかを定めるルールをいう。一義的には各国の国内法がそれぞれのソースルールを定めるが、租税条約の規定によって一部修正される場合がある。

属地主義 territorial taxation principle

組織再編前の期間の欠損金 pre-reorganisation loss

訴訟 lawsuit, litigation

訴訟手続 legal procedure, proceedings

租税委員会（主に OECD の機関を指す） Committee on Fiscal Affairs

租税回避 tax avoidance

租税公課 taxes and other public charges

租税債務 tax liability

租税条約 double taxation convention, double taxation treaty, tax convention, tax treaty

租税条約届出書 application form for income tax convention

租税条約の特典否認ルール subject to tax rule

租税特別措置法 Act on Special Measures concerning Taxation

租税特別措置法施行規則 Regulation for Enforcement of the Act on Special Measures Concerning Taxation

租税特別措置法施行令 Order for Enforcement of Special Measures Concerning Taxation

租税法 tax law

租税法律主義 principle of legality of taxation

その他資本剰余金 other capital reserve, other capital surplus

それぞれに respectively

損益通算 aggregation of profit and loss

損益取引 profit and loss transaction

損害賠償金 compensation for damage

損害保険 non-life insurance

損金 deductible expenses (for tax purposes)

損金経理 making an entry of the amount as expenses for accounting purposes

損金算入できる allowable, deductible

損金算入配当 deductible dividend

損金算入範囲 allowance

損金の額に算入する deduct

損金不算入 exclusion from deductible expense

損金不算入とする exclude from deductible expense

損金不算入とする（主に受け身で） disallow

損金不算入となる disallowable

損金不算入の non-deductible

損失 loss

損失（～から生じた） loss from

損失（～における） loss for

損失（～に係る） loss on

損失申告書 final return in case of loss

尊属 ascendant

た

第一の柱 Pillar 1 [one]

第二の柱 Pillar 2 [two]

対応的調整 correlative adjustment, corresponding adjustment

対価 consideration

第三者 third party

第三者間取引 uncontrolled transaction

第三者間の uncontrolled

代襲相続 succession per stirpes

代襲相続人 successor per stirpes

対象となる（課税などの） subject to

退職 resignation, retirement

退職給与規定 retirement allowance policy

退職金 retirement allowance, retirement benefit, severance pay(ment) 注 severance pay(ment)は会社都合の場合の退職金支給に使用されることが多い。

退職所得 retirement income

退職所得控除額 amount of deduction for retirement income

退職所得の源泉徴収票 retirement income withholding record

退職所得の受給に関する申告書 application concerning receipt of retirement income

退職する retire

退職手当金 retirement allowance

退職手当等とみなす一時金 lump-sum payment regarded as retirement allowance

退職年金 retirement pension

代替的最小課税 alternative minimum tax

第二次納税義務 secondary tax liability

滞納 delinquency

滞納（税金の） tax delinquency

滞納した delinquent

滞納している delinquent, in arrears

滞納者 delinquent taxpayer

滞納処分 procedure for collection of delinquent tax

代表者（法人の） representative

代表者印 representative's seal

代表取締役 managing director, representative director

タイブレイカールール tiebreaker rule

大法人 large corporation

代理人 agent

代理人 PE agent PE

宅地の評価 valuation of residential site

多国籍企業 multinational enterprise

立退料 compensation for removal

タックス・スペアリング・クレジット tax sparing credit 解説 外国で生じた所得について、実際はその所得について現地の税が軽減・免除されているにもかかわらず、居住地国においてその課税がされたものとして、その仮の課税額について行われる特殊な外国税額控除。租税条約に規定がある場合にのみ適用がある。

タックスイコライゼーション tax equalisation 解説 海外赴任者の給与を手取りベースで保証するために導入されるみなし税金（→hypo tax 参照）について、その年中に生じた扶養等の変動要素を考慮して年度末に再計算を行い、差額の精算を行う手続きをいう。法令上の定めではなく、海外出向者の人事・労務の実務として行われている。

タックスヘイブン tax haven

タックスヘイブン（対策）税制 controlled foreign corporation rules (CFC rules)

タックスホリデー tax holiday 解説 特定の産業の発展を企図して、その産業に従事することで得られる所得について一定期間税を免除する政策をいう。

脱税 tax evasion

脱税者 tax evader

脱税をした者 tax evader

建物 building

建物（土地や付属物も含まれている） premises

建物附属設備 building accessories

建物附属設備（賃借物件改良費用） leasehold improvement

たばこ税 tobacco tax

単一性の原則 principle of uniqueness

嘆願（書） petition

嘆願する petition

短期外貨建債権 short-term receivable in foreign currency

短期外貨建債務 short-term debt in foreign currency

短期譲渡所得 capital gains from a transfer of asset held for five years or less

単純承認 absolute acceptance of inheritance

担当者 person in charge

担保 security

ち

地上権 surface right

知的障害者 intellectually disabled person

地方債 Japanese municipal bonds

地方自治体 local government

地方消費税 local consumption tax

地方税法 Local Tax Act [Law]

地方法人税 local corporate tax

地方法人特別税 local special corporate tax

嫡出子 legitimate child

中央値 median

中間申告 interim (tax) return

中間申告書 interim (tax) return

中間納付 interim payment

駐在員事務所 representative office

忠実義務 duty of loyalty

中小企業者等 small and medium (-sized) enterprise 注 中小法人との違いは個別に説明しなければならない。

中小法人 small and medium (-sized) enterprise 注 中小企業者等との違いは個別に説明しなければならない。

注文書 purchase order

超 more than

弔慰金 condolence money

超過税率 higher-than-standard tax rate

長期外貨建債権 long-term receivable in foreign currency

長期外貨建債務 long-term debt in foreign currency

長期借入金 long-term loan payable

長期譲渡所得 capital gains from a transfer of asset held for more than five years

長期棚上債権 long-term suspended claims

調査 audit

調査する examine

徴収する levy

徴収猶予 postponement of collection

調整対象固定資産 fixed asset subject to adjustment

帳簿及び請求書等の保存 maintenance of books and invoices etc.

帳簿価額 book value, carrying amount

帳簿価額の一部評価減 write down

帳簿価額の全額評価減 write off

帳簿書類の整理保存 maintenance of books and records

直接外国税額控除 direct foreign tax credit

直前に immediately 例 immediately previous fiscal year（直前の事業年度）

直前の immediate

著作権 copyright

直系尊属 lineal ascendant

賃金台帳 payroll, payroll book

賃借 lease

賃借権 right of lease

賃借料 rent

賃貸 lease

賃貸借契約 lease agreement [contract]

賃貸借契約書 lease agreement, tenancy agreement

賃貸料 rent

賃貸料収入 rental income

陳腐化した obsolete

つ

通勤 commute

通勤手当 commutation allowance

通勤費用 commuting expense

通常の賃貸料 reasonable rent

通常の賃貸料（小規模住宅等に係る） reasonable rent for small-scale dwelling

通常の賃貸料（使用人に貸与した住宅等に係る） reasonable rent for dwellings etc. leased to an employee

通達 circular, directive, ruling

通知書 notification

続く subsequent

て

（価格、金額等が）で at 例 at a significantly low value 著しく低い価格で

DCF法 discounted cash flow method

定額控除 fixed amount deduction

定額控除限度額 lump-sum exempt amount

低額譲渡 transfer of asset at extraordinary low price

定額法（減価償却方法） straight-line method

低価法 lower of cost and net realisable value

定款 articles of incorporation, constitution, memorandum of association

定期積金 instalment deposits, periodical deposits

定期積金の給付補てん金等 compensation money for benefits from installment deposits, etc.

定期同額給与 regular fixed remuneration

提供を受けた役務 service provided [rendered]

定時株主総会 general shareholder meeting

停止条件 condition precedent

提出 filing, submission

提出期限 filing deadline, filing due date

提出期限の延長 filing extention

提出する file, submit

低税率国［地域］ low tax jurisdiction

抵当権 mortgage

定率法（減価償却の） reducing balance method

適格合併 qualified merger, tax-qualified merger

適格株式移転 qualified share transfer, tax-qualified share transfer

適格株式交換 qualified share for share exchange, tax-qualified share for share exchange

適格株式分配 tax-qualified share dividend

適格居住者 qualified resident

適格現物出資 qualified capital contribution in kind, tax-qualified contribution in kind

適格現物分配 qualified distribution in kind, tax-qualified distribution in kind

適格ストックオプション qualified stock option

適格組織再編成 qualified corporate reorganisation

適格分割 qualified company split, tax-qualified company split

適切な adequate, appropriate, relevant

適用対象金額 eligible income

手数料 commission

デミニミス基準 de minimis rule 解説 法律などの規定が適用される最低ラインをいい、そのラインを下回るものについてはその規定が適用されないという基準をいう。"de minimis" とは、ラテン語で「些細なことについて」という意味。

デリバティブ取引 derivative transaction

転換社債 convertible bond

電気通信利用役務 electronic service(s)

電気通信利用役務の提供 services provided via electronic and telecommunication networks

電子申告 electronic filing

電磁的方法 electromagnetic means

電信売相場 telegraphic transfer selling rate

電信買相場 telegraphic transfer buying rate

電信相場の中値 telegraphic transfer middle rate

と

問屋 commission agent, commissionaire

同一生計配偶者 spouse living in the same household as the earner of salary

統括国税調査官（日本の税務当局の役職） chief examiner

登記 registration

登記官 registrar

当期純利益 net income

登記する register

同居特別障害者 persons with special disabilities living together with the salary earner

同居老親等 elderly parents living together with the salary earner, etc.

当座借越 overdraft

動産 movable property

当事者 party

投資信託 investment trust

同時の contemporaneous

同時文書化 contemporaneous documentation

同族会社 family company

同族株主 family shareholder

盗難 robbery, theft

道府県税事務所 prefectural tax office

道府県民税 prefectural tax

登録 entry, record, registration

登録（権利などの） recordation

登録国外事業者 registered foreign business

登録する enter, record, register

登録免許税 registration and license tax, registration duty

特定遺贈 specified devise

特定役務の提供 provision of specific services

特定課税仕入れ specific taxable purchase

特定期間（消費税法の） specified period

特定口座（株式等の） specific account

特定資産の譲渡等 transfer of specific assets, etc.

特定受益証券発行信託 specified beneficiary securities issuing trust

特定同族会社 specific family company

特定納税義務者 specified taxpayer

特定扶養親族 specific dependents

特定目的会社 Tokutei Mokuteki Kaisha (TMK)

特定目的信託 special purpose trust

特定役員 specified officer

特定役員退職手当等 specified officer retirement allowance etc.

特典制限条項 limitation on benefits provision

特別控除 special deduction

特別国税調査官（日本の税務当局の役職） special examiner

特別障害者 persons with special disabilities

特別償却 special depreciation

特別清算 special liquidation

特別徴収（個人住民税の） special collection (of individual inhabitant tax)

特別徴収義務者 special collecting agent

特別の寄与 special contribution

特別目的会社 special purpose company

匿名組合 Tokumei Kumiai, anonymous association, sleeping partnership

独立価格比準法 Comparable Uncontrolled Price Method (CUP method)

独立企業間価格 arm's length price (ALP)

独立企業間価格算定手法 transfer pricing methodology

独立企業間価格幅 arm's length range

独立企業原則 arm's length principle (ALP)

独立代理人 independent agent

独立取引比準法 Comparable Uncontrolled Transaction Method

土地課税台帳 land tax register book

土地再評価差額金（評価益） net unrealised gain on land revaluation

土地再評価差額金（評価損） net unrealised loss on land revaluation

土地の上に存する権利 right on land

都庁 Tokyo Metropolitan Government Office

特許権 patent (right)

届出 notification

都民税 metropolitan inhabitant tax

トリーティオーバーライド treaty override
解説 既存の租税条約の規定の内容に抵触する国内法を立法し、執行することをいう。アメリカのような後法優先を原則とする国においては、後で成立した国内法の規定によって既存の条約の規定が無効化されてしまうといったことが起こり得る。

トリーティショッピング treaty shopping
解説 有利な租税条約の恩典を享受することのみを目的に経済的に合理性のない取引を作出すること。

取極め agreement, arrangement

取消し avoidance, cancellation, disaffirmance, disaffirmation, revocation

取り消す avoid, cancel, disaffirm, invalidate, rescind, revoke

取締役 member of board of directors

取締役会議事録 minutes of board of directors' meeting

取引相場のない株式 stock without quotation

取引単位営業利益法 transactional net margin method (TNMM)

と

な

内国普通法人等の設立の届出　Notification of Establishment of Domestic Ordinary Corporation

内国法人　domestic corporation [company]

内部取引（本支店間及び支店間の取引）　internal dealing

内部取引（本支店間及び支店間の取引又は同一法人内部の原価計算や減価償却等）　internal transaction

に

二国間 APA　bilateral APA

二国間の　bilateral

二重課税　double taxation

二重課税の排除　double tax(ation) relief

二重居住者　dual resident

二重目的テスト　dual purpose test

二段階アプローチ　two-step approach

日勤手当　day-duty allowance

日当　per diem

日本銀行　Bank of Japan

日本国籍　Japanese nationality [citizenship]

日本国内源泉所得　Japan source income

入湯税　bathing tax

任意組合　Nin-i Kumiai

任意償却　voluntary depreciation

任意調査　tax audit, tax audit on a voluntary basis

任意積立金　voluntary reserve

任意の　optional

認識　recognition

認識する　recognise

認定 NPO 法人　certified NPOs

認定 NPO 法人等寄附金特別控除　special credit for contributions to certified NPOs

ね

ネクサス　nexus　解説 納税をする国・地域と納税者の地理的なつながりをいう。

年金　pension

年金基金　pension fund

年金事務所　Japan Pension Service Branch Office

年金受給者　pensioner

年金制度　pension plan, pension scheme

年次株主総会　annual shareholder meeting

年末調整　year-end adjustment

年末調整のための給与所得控除後の給与等の金額の表　Table of Salary Amounts after Employment Income Deductions for the Year-end Adjustment

年末調整のための算出所得税額の速算表　Quick Calculating Income Tax Amount Table for the Year-end Adjustment

の

納期限の延長 extension of tax payment due date, extension of time to pay tax, payment extension

納期の特例（源泉所得税） special provision for due date for withholding income tax

納税額 tax due

納税管理人 tax agent

納税義務 obligation to pay tax, tax liability, tax obligation

納税義務者 taxable person

納税告知書 notification (form) of tax payment

納税者番号 taxpayer identification number

納税証明書 certificate of tax payment

納税地 place of [for] tax payment

納税地の指定 designation of place for tax payment

納税の告知 notification of tax payment

納税の猶予 grace of tax payment

納税の猶予制度 grace system of tax payment

ノウハウ know how

納付（税金などの） payment

納付過少 underpayment

納付期限 payment deadline, payment due, payment due date

納付告知書 tax notice

納付書 tax payment slip

納付すべき税額 tax liability

能力 competence

能力を有する competent

のれん goodwill

は

パートナー（組合の） partner

パートナーシップ partnership

バイアウト支払 buy-out payment **解説** 費用分担契約の参加者がその契約を途中で脱退することとなった場合に、形成途中の無形資産に係る持分を他の参加者に譲渡することにつき受領する対価をいう。移転価格税制の文脈で使用される。

バイイン支払 buy-in payment **解説** 費用分担契約に中途から参加しようとする者が、それまでの費用分担契約の成果に対する持分を取得することにつき支払う対価をいう。移転価格税制の文脈で使用される。

売価還元法 retail method

売却益 gain on sale (of ～)

配偶者 spouse

配偶者控除 exemption for spouses

配偶者控除（贈与税の） deduction of gift tax for spouse

配偶者特別控除 special exemption for spouses

賠償する indemnify

バイセル契約 buy-sell agreement **解説** 外資系企業がその関連会社と締結する契約の形態。自らが関連会社から仕入れた商品の販売主体となって、その販売に係る収益及び費用を認識する。

配当（金） dividend

配当還元方式 dividend discount method

配当控除 credit for dividends

配当所得 dividend income

配当等の所得税徴収高計算書 Statement (tax payment slip) of Income Tax Collected from Dividends, etc.

売買目的有価証券 securities held for trading

配賦 allocation

配賦可能な allocable

配賦方法 allocation method

ハイブリッド事業体 hybrid entity **解説** 国によって課税上の取扱いが変わってしまう事業体をいう。米国税制上透明な事業体とされるLLCなどが挙げられる。

ハイポタックス hypothetical tax **解説** 海外赴任者が仮に海外赴任しなかったとした場合に得られるであろう手取りベースの給与の額を計算するために算定される架空の所得税、社会保険料等の控除額をいう。手取り給与額は海外赴任者の海外での給与額を決定する際の基礎データとするために計算されるため、この架空の控除額については法律上の納税・納付義務はない。

バイラテラルAPA bilateral advance pricing arrangement **解説** 二国間の権限のある当局の間で行われる事前確認をいう。

場所 site

端数切捨て rounding off

パススルー事業体 pass-through businesses（主に複数形で用いる）, pass-through entity

パススルーの pass-through **解説** 収益及び費用が事業体に帰属せず、その構成員（出資者等）に対してその出資比率等に応じて配分されること。その事業体は納税主体とはならず、収益及び費用の配分を受けた構成員において所得の計算及び申告を行うことになる。

罰金 fine, penalty charge

発行済株式 outstanding shares, outstanding stocks

発行済の outstanding

発生主義 accrual basis

発送基準 shipping basis

パテントボックス patent box **解説** 特許料その他一定の無形資産の対価として稼得される所得に対して軽減された税率で課税する制度。欧州に導入国が多い。

範囲外 out of the scope

判決 decision, judgement

版権 copyright

判示 ruling

販売基準 sales basis

販売費 selling expenses

販売費及び一般管理費 selling, general and administrative expenses

判例 case, judicial precedent

判例法 case law

ひ

BEAT Base Erosion and Anti-abuse Tax

非永住者 non-permanent resident

比較可能性 comparability

比較可能性分析 comparability analysis

比較可能な comparable

比較対象企業 comparable company, comparables（複数形で）

非課税 tax exemption

非課税売上 non-taxable sales

非課税財産 non-taxable assets

非課税所得 non-taxable income

非課税通勤手当 non-taxable commutation allowance

非課税取引 non-taxable transaction

非課税の non-taxable, tax-exempt, tax free

非課税文書（印紙税の） non-taxable document for stamp duty

被合併法人 predecessor corporation, transferor corporation

非関連者 unrelated corporation, unrelated party, unrelated person

引当金 allowance (for ～), provision (for ～)

引継ぎ succession

引き継ぐ succeed

非居住外国人 expatriate, non-resident alien

非居住者 non-resident, alien（主に米国）

非居住者・外国法人の所得についての所得税徴収高計算書 Statement (tax payment slip) of Income Tax Collected from Income of a Non-Resident/Foreign Corporation

非居住者等に支払われる組合契約に基づく利益の支払調書 Report of Payment for Profits Under a Partnership Contract to Be Paid to Non-Residents

非居住制限納税義務者 non-resident taxpayer with limitation

非居住被相続人 non-resident ancestor

非居住無制限納税義務者 non-resident taxpayer without limitation

引渡基準 delivery basis

引渡し delivery

非経常取引 non-routine transaction

非公開会社 private company

被支配 controlled

非上場株式 unlisted stock

被相続人 ancestor

卑属 descendant

非嫡出子 child out of marriage

非適格合併 non tax-qualified merger

非適格株式移転 non tax-qualified share transfer

非適格株式交換 non tax-qualified share for share exchange

非適格株式分配 non tax-qualified share dividend

非適格現物出資 non tax-qualified contribution in kind

非適格現物分配 non tax-qualified distribution in kind

非適格の non-qualified

非適格分割 non tax-qualified company split

一人当たり per capita

ひとり親控除　exemption for single parents

備品　fixture, furnishment, furniture

備忘価額　memorandum value

183 日ルール　183-day rule

費用　expense

評価する（賦課課税方式の税制度の国においては、税務当局が確定納税額を算定すること）　assess

評価方法（～の）　valuation method of ～

費用収益対応の原則　principle of matching cost with revenue

標準　standard

標準原価　standard cost

標準税率　standard tax rate

費用分担契約　cost contribution arrangement (CCA), cost sharing arrangement (CSA)

表面税率　nominal tax rate

比例して　pro rata

ふ

ファントムストック　phantom stock
解説 業績連動報酬の一つ。役員、従業員に対して架空の株式をその時の時価で交付し、権利確定時の時価で精算して現金を給付する報酬制度をいう。疑似的な持分に対応する配当金という形での給付もある。

賦課　imposition

賦課課税制度　official assessment system

付加価値税　value added tax

付加価値割　added value portion of enterprise tax

賦課決定通知書（固定資産税などの）　tax notice (of assessment)

不可抗力　force majeure

付加税　surcharge, surtax

不均一課税適用法人　corporation subject to different taxation

含み益　unrealised (capital) gain

含み損　unrealised (capital) loss

福利厚生施設　welfare facility

付随費用　incidental cost

附属明細書　supplementary statement

附帯税　accessory tax

負担付贈与　onerous gift

普通株式　common share, common stock, ordinary share, ordinary stock

普通償却　ordinary depreciation

普通預金　ordinary account

復興特別所得税　restoration special income tax

物納　payment of tax in kind

不動産　immovable property, real property

不動産鑑定士　real estate appraiser, real estate surveyor

不動産関連法人　real property holding corporation

不動産関連法人株式の譲渡　transfer of shares issued by a real property holding corporation

不動産取得税　real estate [property] acquisition tax

不動産所得　real estate income

船荷証券　bill of landing

不納付加算税　additional tax on nonpayment of withholding tax, late payment charge (for withholding tax)

不服（行政処分に対する）　administrative complaint

不服申立て　tax appeal

不服申立て前置主義　principle of petition after administrative complaint

不服申立てをする　appeal administrative complaint

部分課税対象金額　partially taxable income

部分適用対象金額　partially eligible income

不法所得　illegal income

扶養控除　exemption for dependents

扶養親族　dependent(s)

プライベートルーリング　private ruling **解説** 個々の納税者が税務当局と個別に合意した租税に関する取扱いをいう。通常は、その合意に係る納税者についてのみ有効とされる。

フリーレント　free rent

フリーレントの　rent-free

振替納税　tax payment by transfer account

プリザベーション条項　preservation clause **解説** 租税条約によって国内法より重い課税を受けることはないという租税条約の基本原理。

ふるさと納税　contributions to prefectural and municipality governments (or "Furusato Nozei")

フロースルー（＝パススルー）事業体　flow-through entity **解説** フロースルー（パススルー）の事業体。

フロースルー（＝パススルー）の　flow-through **解説** →「パススルーの」を参照

プロラタ　pro rata

分割基準　basis of proration for local tax

分割払い　instalment plan

文書化　documentation

文書回答（税務当局の）　letter ruling

粉飾決算　window dressing

分離課税　separate assessment

分離課税方式　separate assessment system

へ

平均　mean

丙欄　column C

ペーパーカンパニー　paper company, shell company

ベストメソッドルール　best method rule **解説** 移転価格税制で、国外関連取引ごとに最もふさわしい独立企業間価格算定手法を適用すること。

別表（申告書の）　schedule

別表（法令の）　appended table

BEPS防止措置実施条約　Multilateral Convention to Implement Tax Treaty Related Measures to Prevent Base Erosion and Profit Shifting (Multilateral Instrument)

ベリーレシオ　berry ratio **解説** 移転価格税制における価格算定方法の一つ。売上総利益÷販売費及び一般管理で求められる。

返還（収入した補助金などの）　repayment

返還する（収入した補助金などを）　repay

変更　change in ～

弁護士　attorney, lawer

ベンチマーク　benchmark **解説** 移転価格税制において、国外関連取引における利益率の妥当性を検証するために比較対象企業の財務データを抽出すること。

ベンチマーク分析　benchmark analysis **解説** ベンチマーク（→ベンチマークの解説参照）により抽出された比較対象企業の利益率に一定の統計的処理を施して適正利益率の範囲を算出する一連の行為を指す。

ベンチマークレポート　benchmarking report **解説** 移転価格税制で、ベンチマークによって算定された独立企業間価格を報告するレポート。移転価格文書の一部。

返品　returned goods

弁理士　patent attorney

ほ

法　law

法（的）形式　legal form

法（的）形態　legal form

包括遺贈　comprehensive devise

包括受遺者　comprehensive legatee

法規　regulation

報酬　consideration, remuneration

報酬・料金等の所得税徴収高計算書　Statement (tax payment slip) of Income Tax Collected from Remuneration/Fees, etc.

法人　corporate body, legal person

法人課税信託　trust subject to corporate tax

法人事業税　corporate business tax

法人住民税　corporate inhabitant tax

法人税　corporate (income) tax (CIT)

法人税基本通達　Commissioner's Directive on Corporate Income Tax Act

法人税の申告書　corporate (income) tax return

法人税法　Corporation Tax Act [Law]

法人税法施行規則　Regulation for Enforcement of the Corporation Tax Act

法人税法施行令　Order for the Enforcement of the Corporation Tax Act

法人税割　corporation levy

法人の　corporate

法人番号　corporate number

法定換算方法　default translation method

法定減価償却方法　default depreciation method

法定実効税率　statutory tax rate

法定準備金　legal reserve, statutory reserve

法定償却　statutory depreciation

法定税率　statutory tax rate

法定相続人　hair at law, legal hair, legal successor

法定相続分　legal share of legacy

法定耐用年数　statutory useful life

法定調書合計表　totalised table of statutory records

法定の　default, statutory

法定納期限　statutory due date for tax payment

法定のものでない　non-default

法定福利費　legal welfare cost [expense]

法定利息　statutory interest

法的所有権　legal procedure, legal title

法的手続　legal procedure, proceedings（複数形）

法的な　legal

法的に　legally

法的二重課税　judicial double taxation

法的要件　legal requirement

法の濫用　abuse of law

法律　law, legislation

法律意見　legal opinion

法律上の　juridical, legislative

法律的な　juridical

法令　laws and ordinances, ordinance, statute

法令遵守　compliance

法令を遵守した　compliant

法令を遵守する　comply (with)

簿外資産　unrecorded asset

簿外負債　unrecorded liability

保険　insurance

保険金　insurance (money)

保険金控除　deduction for insurance proceed

保険契約　insurance contract

保険差益 gain on insurance claim

保険証（健康保険の被保険者証） certificate of participation in health insurance

保険証券 insurance policy

保険料 (insurance) premium

保険料控除申告書 application for insurance premium deduction

保護する（法律上） indemnify

保守主義の原則 principle of conservatism

保証金 security deposit

補償調整 compensating adjustment

補助金 grant

補助的活動 auxiliary activity

補助的な auxiliary

保税倉庫 bonded warehouse

保税地域 bonded area

保全差押 preservative seizure

北海道庁 Hokkaido Government

本社 head office, headquarters

本税 principal tax

本店 head office, headquarters

本人（代理人との関係で） principal

本人確認書類 documents for identification of the individual

ま

マークアップ　mark-up　解説 原価・費用に対して利益を上乗せすることを指す。

マーケティング無形資産　marketing intangible

マージン　margin

毎月の　monthly

マイナンバー　My Number

マイナンバーカード　My Number Card

前　before

前受収益　deferred revenue

前金　advance

前に　previous

前払い　advance

前払費用　prepaid expense

マスターファイル　master file

マネーロンダリング　money laundering

マネジメントフィー　management fee

満期日　maturity date

満期保有目的債券　head-to-maturity bond

み

未収還付消費税等　consumption tax receivable

未収還付法人税　corporate (income) tax receivable

未償却残高　undepreciated balance

満たす　suffice

見積り耐用年数　estimated useful life

みなし申告（中間申告の）　deemed declaration

みなし税額控除　tax sparing credit

みなし税（金）　hypothetical tax

みなし相続財産　deemed inherited assets

みなし贈与財産　deemed gift

みなし配当　deemed dividend

ミニマムタックス　minimum tax　解説 OECD における残された BEPS 防止措置における第二の柱で決定された措置。実効税率が 15 % を下回る場合に、その差分について最終的な親会社に課される上乗せ課税。

未納税金　tax liability

未払いの　outstanding, payable

未払法人税　corporate (income) tax payable

未払消費税等　consumption tax payable

未分割遺産　undivided bequest

未満　less than

民事再生法　Civil Rehabilitation Act

民法　Civil Law

む

無額面株式　no-par (value) share [stock]

無期限に　indefinitely

無形固定資産　intangible fixed asset

無形資産　intangible asset, intangible property, intangibles

無限責任社員　general partner

無差別条項　non-discrimination provision

無償譲渡　voluntary conveyance

無申告加算金　late filing charge (for local tax)

無申告加算税　late filing tax (for national tax)

無対価組織再編成　corporate reorganisation without consideration

まみむ

無利息貸付け　interest-free loan

め

名義株　dummy stock

明細　schedule

明瞭性の原則　principle of clarity

免除　cancellation, exemption, relief

免除された　exempt, exempted

免除する　exempt, relieve

免税売上（消費税法）　exempt sales

免税事業者（消費税の）　exempt business

免税点　tax exemption limit

も

持分　interset

モデル租税条約　model tax convention

元帳　ledger

漏れた　fail to

や

夜勤手当 night-duty allowance

役員給与 director's compensation [remuneration, salary]

役員賞与 director's bonus

役員退職慰労金 director's retirement allowance [benefit]

役員に貸与した住宅等に係る通常の賃貸料の額 normal rent for dwellings etc. leased to a director

約定利息 agreed interest

ゆ

有価証券 securities

有給休暇 paid leave

遊休資産 non-operating asset

優遇税制 preferential tax treatment

有形固定資産 tangible fixed asset

有限会社 Yugen Kaisha

有限責任会社 limited liability company

有限責任組合 limited liability partnership, limited partnership

有限責任社員 limited partner

優先株式 preferred share, preferred stock

郵便貯金 postal savings, post-office savings

郵便で by post

猶予 postponement

猶予期間 grace period

輸出免税売上 export exemption sales

ユニラテラル APA unilateral advance pricing arrangement 解説 一国の税務当局との間で国外関連取引につき確認を受けることをいう。相互協議を伴わないため、他方の国での課税リスクは残存する。

ユニット・トラスト unit trust 解説 投資信託の一種。イギリスやその他旧英連邦国を中心にした一部の国で法律に基づき組成される。ユニットトラストの受益権には日本の税法上外国投資信託として扱われるものも存在するが、実際の分類に当たってはユニットトラストごとに信託行為の検討を要する。

輸入統計品目表 statistical code for import 解説 実行関税率表のこと。

よ

用益権 usufruct

預金 cash in bank

翌課税期間（消費税等の） next taxable period

翌期 next period

預貯金 money in bank account

予定納税 estimated tax prepayment, provisional tax payment

予納 prepayment

予約レート（為替） forward (exchange) rate

より少ない less

ら

来期　next period

濫用防止　anti-abuse

り

リース　lease

リース契約　lease agreement [contract]

リース債務　lease obligation

リースの貸手　lessor

リースの借手　lessee

利益準備金　legal retained earnings, retained earnings reserve

利益剰余金　retained earnings

利益水準指標　profit level indicator

利益積立金額　profit reserve

利益の上乗せ部分　mark-up

利益比準法　Comparable Profit Method (CPM)

利益分割法　profit split method

利ざや　margin

利子　interest

理事（社団法人・財団法人の）　director

利子所得　interest income

利子税　interest tax

利子等の所得税徴収高計算書　Statement (tax payment slip) of income tax collected from interest, etc.

リスク　risk

リスク限定販売会社　limited risk distributor

リストリクテッドストック　restricted stock
解説　譲渡制限付株式のこと。

立証責任　onus of proof

立法　legislation

立法上の　legislative

リバースチャージ方式　reverse charge mechanism

留保　retain

留保金課税　taxation on undistributed profit

領収書　receipt

療養　recuperation

臨場［実地］税務調査　field tax audit

る

類似業種比準法　comparable industry method

累進課税　graduated taxation, progression

累進税率　graduated tax rates, progressive tax rates

累進税率の各税率区分　bracket

れ

暦年　calendar year

連結　consolidation

連結（法人税）申告書　consolidated (corporate) tax return

連結財務諸表　consolidated financial statement

連結する　consolidate

連結納税　tax consolidation

連結納税制度　consolidated tax return filing system, tax consolidation system

連邦税　federal (income) tax（米国）

連絡調整官（日本の税務当局の役職）　co-ordination officer

ろ

ロイヤルティ　royalty

老人控除対象配偶者　elderly spouses covered by exemption

老人扶養親族　elderly dependents

労働基準法　Labour Standards Act

労働保険　labour insurance

ローカルファイル　local file

ロールバック　rollback　解説　事前確認申請によって確認された独立企業間価格の算定方法その他の事項が、その事前確認申請に係る期間より前の事業年度にも遡及して適用されること。

六親等内の親族　any person within sixth degree of relationship by consanguinity

ロケーションセービング　location saving

わ

和解　settlement

和解契約　settlement agreement

渡切り交際費　entertainment expense paid in lump sum

割引債の償還金　profit on redemption amount of discount bonds

割引債の償還差益　profit from redemption of discount bonds

【税務辞典】 英和編
English ➡ Japanese

A

abuse of law　法の濫用

accessory tax　附帯税

account　口座、勘定

account receivable　売掛金

accounting audit　会計監査

accounting documents　計算書類

accounting period　会計期間

accounting principles　会計原則

accounting standards　会計基準

accrual basis　発生主義

accumulated depreciation　減価償却累計額

accumulated tax losses　税務上の繰越欠損金の合計

acquisition cost　取得価額、取得費

addition　加算

additional levy　加算金

additional paid-in capital　（主に米国）株主からの払込金額のうち株式の額面金額を超える部分の金額

additional tax　加算税

adjustment for taxable income　税務調整

adjustment of final return　申告調整

administration of the settlement [liquidation]　清算事務

administrative action　行政行為

administrative circular　行政通達

administrative complaint　不服（行政処分に対する）

administrative direction　行政指導

administrative discretion　行政裁量

administrative disposition　行政処分

administrative guidance　行政指導

administrative law　行政法

administrative litigation　行政訴訟

administrative mechanism　機関（社団法人・財団法人の）

administrative power　行政権

Administrative Procedure Act　行政手続法

administrative remedy　行政救済

administrator of bequest　遺産管理人

advance　前金、前払い

advance price agreement　事前確認申請 [米]

advance price arrangement　事前確認申請

advance ruling　事前照会制度

advanced depreciation　圧縮記帳

AEOI　→ Automatic Exchange of Infromation

affiliate　関連会社

affiliate(d) company [corporation]　関連会社

after　（～より）後

after tax　税引き後

agent　代理人

agent PE　代理人 PE

aggregation of profit and loss　損益通算

agreed interest　約定利息

agreement　契約、取決（極）め

alian　非居住者（主に米国）

alianation　譲渡

allocable　配賦可能な

allocation　配賦

allocation method　配賦方法

allowable　損金算入できる

allowance　控除（特に個人所得税における）、損金算入範囲

allowance for bad debt　貸倒引当金

allowance for bonus　賞与引当金

allowance for dismissal without notice in advance 解雇予告手当

ALP → arm's length price、arm's length principle

alternative minimum tax 代替的最小課税

amended (tax) return 修正申告書

amendment 修正申告

amortisation method 減価償却方法（有形減価償却資産以外）

amortisation period 減価償却期間（有形減価償却資産以外）

amount for price adjustment 価格調整金

ancestor 被相続人

annual (tax) return 確定申告書

annual filing 確定申告

annual shareholder meeting 年次株主総会

anonymous association 匿名組合

anti-abuse 濫用防止

AOA OECD 承認アプローチ

appeal 異議申立て

appeal administrative complaint 不服申立てをする

appended table 別表（法令の）

application 申請（税務上の）

application form 申請書

appropriation 充当

appropriation of refunded tax 還付金の充当

arm's length price 独立企業間価格

arm's length principle 独立企業原則

arm's length range 独立企業間価格幅

arrangement 契約

arrangement 取極め

article 条

article(s) of incorporation 定款

article on independent personal services 自由職業者条項

ascendant 尊属

assess 評価する（賦課課税方式の税制度の国においては税務当局が確定納税額を算定すること）

assessment 税額の算定（賦課課税方式の税目に関して税務当局が行うもの）

asset purchased at an unreasonably high value 高価買入資産

associated company [corporation] [emterprise] 関連会社

association or foundation without juridical personality 人格のない社団等

at （価格、金額等が）～で

attachment 差押え

attorney 弁護士

attributable income approach [principle] 帰属主義

auction 競売

audit 監査、調査

audit report 監査報告書

auditing corporation 監査法人

Authorized OECD Approach OECD 承認アプローチ

autograph 署名

Automatic Exchange of Information 自動的情報交換

auxiliary 補助的な

auxiliary activity 補助的活動

avoid 取り消す

avoidance 取消し

B

bad faith 悪意（法律）

Bank of Japan 日本銀行

bank seal　銀行印

Base Erosion and Anti-abuse Tax　税源浸食濫用防止税（米国の税制度の１つ）

Base Erosion and Profit Shifting　税源浸食及び利益の移転

base period　基準期間

base year　基準年度

BEAT　→ Base Erosion and Anti-abuse Tax

before　（～より）前

beginning balance　期首残高

beginning of accounting period　期首

benchmark　ベンチマーク（和英見出し参照）

benchmark analysis　ベンチマーク分析（和英見出し参照）

benchmarking report　ベンチマークレポート（和英見出し参照）

beneficial interest in trust　信託受益権

beneficial owner　恩典の享受者（租税条約の）

beneficiary　受益者（信託の）

benefit in kind　経済的利益（金銭以外の）

benefits in kind　現物給与、現物給付

BEPS (Base Erosion and Profit Shifting)　税源浸食及び利益の移転

bequest　遺産

berry ratio　ベリーレシオ（和英見出し参照）

best method rule　ベストメソッドルール（和英見出し参照）

bilateral　二国間の

bilateral advance pricing arrangement　バイラテラル APA（和英見出し参照）

bill of landing　船荷証券

board of liquidators　清算人会

bona fides　善意（法律）　例 bona fides third party（善意の第三者）

bond issuance expense [cost]　社債発行費

bonded area　保税地域

bonded warehouse　保税倉庫

book value　帳簿価額

border tax adjustment　国境税調整

bracket　累進税率の各税率区分

branch profits tax　支店利益税

browse　閲覧する（固定資産課税台帳など）

building　建物

business judgement rule　経営判断原則

business year　事業年度

buy-in payment　バイイン支払（和英見出し参照）

buy-out payment　バイアウト支払（和英見出し参照）

buy-sell agreement　バイセル契約（和英見出し参照）

by correspondence delivery　信書で

by post　郵便で

C

cabinet order　政令（具体的な政令ではなく一般的に政令というとき）

calendar year　暦年

cancel　取り消す

cancellation　取消し、免除、（株式の）消却

capital　資本金

capital allowance　減価償却費

capital contribution　出資

capital expenditure [expense]　資本的支出

capital gain　譲渡利益

capital gain on exchange of properties　交換差益

capital reserve　資本準備金

capital structure diagram　資本関係図

capital surplus　資本剰余金

capital transaction　資本（等）取引

capitalisation　資産計上

carried forward　（翌来への）繰越

carry　（帳簿に）記帳する

carry back　繰戻し

carrying amount　帳簿価額

carry-over deduction　繰越控除

case　判例

case law　判例法

cash　現金

cash at bank　預金

cash basis　現金主義

cash book　現金出納帳

cash box　キャッシュボックス（和英見出し参照）

cash conversion of property　財産の換価

cash in bank　預金

casualty　災害

caution money　敷金

CbCR　→ Country by Country Report

CCA　→ Cost Contribution Arrangement

certificate　証明書

certificate of a seal-impression　印鑑証明書

certificate of residence　居住者証明

certificate of tax payment　納税証明書

certified NPOs　認定 NPO 法人

certified public accountant　公認会計士

certified tax accountant　税理士

CFC　→ controlled foreign corporation

CFC rules　CFC ルール、外国子会社合算税制（タックスヘイブン対策税制）

change in ～　～の変更

charitable trust　慈善信託

chart of accounts　勘定科目の一覧表

chart of shareholders　資本関係図

child out of marriage　非嫡出子

CIF　（貨物の）運賃・保険料込み価格（条件）

circular　通達

CIT　→ corporate (income) tax

citizenship　国籍

city hall　市役所（建物としての）

city office　市役所

civil law　民法

claim　債権

claim for a tax refund　還付請求

class　種類

class shares　種類株式

closing balance　期末残高

closing date　決算日

closing rate　決算日レート（為替換算のための）

collection of claim　債権の取立て

commentary on the OECD Model Tax Convention　OECD モデル租税条約コメンタリー

commission　（委託）手数料

commission agent　問屋

commissionaire　問屋、コミッショネア

Commissioner's Directive on Operation of Transfer Pricing　移転価格事務運営指針

Committee on Fiscal Affairs　（主に OECD の機関を指して）租税委員会

Common Reporting Standard (CRS)　共通報告基準

common share　普通株式、普通株式

commutation allowance　通勤手当

commute　通勤

commuting expense　通勤費用

company residence　社宅

comparability　比較可能性

comparability analysis　比較可能性分析

comparable　比較可能な（移転価格の文脈で用いられる場合は、第三者取引又は非関連会社が検証対象の取引又は企業と比較可能性を有することを意味する）

comparable company　比較対象企業

comparable profit method (CPM)　利益比準法

comparable uncontrolled price method (CUP)　独立価格比準法

comparable uncontrolled transaction method (CUT)　独立取引比準法

comparables　比較対象企業

compensating adjustment　補償調整

compensation for damage　損害賠償金

compensation for expense and loss　経費補助金

compensation for removal　立退料

compensation for revenue　収益保証金

competence　能力、権限

competent　能力を有する、権限のある

competent authority　権限のある当局

completed construction method　工事完成基準

completion of liquidation　清算結了

compliance　法令遵守

compliant　法令を遵守した

comply (with)　法令を遵守する

compulsory execution　強制執行

compulsory tax investigation　強制調査

computation　計算する

compute　計算

conceal　隠蔽する

concealment　隠蔽

condition precedent　停止条件

condition subsequent　解除条件

condolence money　弔慰金

confidentiality (obligation)　守秘義務

consideration　対価、報酬

consideration for the transfer of land, etc. located in Japan　国内にある土地等の譲渡による対価

consideration in kind　現物対価、現物報酬

consign　委託する

consignee　受託者（委託業務の）

consigner　委託者

consignment　委託

consolidate　連結する

consolidated (corporate) tax return　連結（法人税）申告書

consolidated financial statement　連結財務諸表

consolidated tax return filing system　連結納税制度

consolidation　連結

constituent　構成する

constituent entity　構成企業

constitution　憲法、定款

constitutional　憲法（上）の

contemporaneous　同時の

contemporaneous documentation　同時文書化

contingent liability　偶発債務

contract　契約、契約書、請負

contract agreement　請負契約

contract manufacturer　受託製造業者

contract manufacturing　製造請負

contract of merger　合併契約書

contract service　サービス受託

contract service provider　役務受託者

contractual　契約上の

contribute　拠出する、出資する

contribution　出資、拠出（社会保険などに対する）

contribution in kind　現物出資

contribution to social security　社会保険料

control 支配する

controlled 支配される、被支配

controlled foreign corporation [company] (CFC) 外国関係会社

controlled transaction 国外関連取引

controlling 支配している

convention 条約、協約

convertible bond 転換社債

copyright 著作権、版権

corporate 法人の

corporate (income) tax 法人税

corporate (income) tax payable 未払法人税

corporate (income) tax receivable 未収還付法人税

corporate (income) tax return 法人税の申告書

corporate body 法人

corporate bonds 社債

corporate inversion コーポレートインバージョン 解説 組織再編行為の一種で、企業グループが外国に親会社となる会社を設立すること。この親会社は低税率国に設立されることが多く、特に租税回避の観点から問題となる。

corporate reorganisation without consider-ation 無対価組織再編成

corporation in the public interest 公益法人

corporation seal 会社印、角印

correct 更正する

correction (of ～) 更正

correction notice 更正通知書

correction of prior period errors 誤謬修正（過去年度の会計数値の）

correlative adjustment 対応的調整

corresponding adjustment 対応的調整

cost accounting 原価計算

cost contribution arrangement 費用分担契約

cost of living 生計費

cost plus agreement [contract] コストプラス（契約）

cost plus method (CPM) 原価基準法

cost sharing arrangement [agreement] (CSA) 費用分担契約

cost variance 原価差額

Country by Country Report 国別報告事項

country of residence [domicile] 居住地国

CPM → cost plus method、comparable profits method

credit 税額控除する、貸方記帳する

credit balance 貸方残高

credit method 外国税額控除方式

creditable foreign tax 控除対象外国法人税

creditor 貸方、債権者

CRS → Common Reporting Standards

CSA → cost sharing arrangement

cumulative tax losses 税務上の繰越欠損金の合計

CUP method → comparable uncontrolled price method

currency forward contract 為替予約

customer acceptance basis 検収基準

customer('s) acceptance standards 検収基準

customs 関税、税関

customs duties 関税

customs value 関税評価額

CUT method → comparable uncontrolled transaction method

C

D

D

date of enforcement　施行日

date stamp　消印

day-duty allowance　日勤手当

DCF　→ discounted cash flow

de facto marital relationship　事実婚

de minimis　最低基準

de minimis rule　デミニミスルール（和英見出し参照）

deadline　期限（申告・納税の）

debenture　社債

debit　借方

debit balance　借方残高

debt in foreign currency　外貨建債務

debtor　借方、債務者

decision　判決、裁決

declaration　申告

declaratory stipulation　宣言規定

declare　申告する

deduct　控除する（所得から）、損金の額に算入する

deductible　控除できる（所得から）、損金算入できる

deductible dividend　損金算入配当

deductible expenses　損金

deductible limit of amortisation amount　減価償却限度額（有形減価償却資産以外）

deductible limit of depreciation amount　減価償却限度額（有形減価償却資産）

deduction for social insurance premiums　社会保険料控除

deemed declaration　みなし申告（中間申告の）

deemed dividend　みなし配当

deemed inherited assets　みなし相続財産

default　法定の、債務不履行

default depreciation method　法定減価償却方法

default translation method　法定換算方法

deferred expense　繰延資産

deferred payment of income tax　延納（確定申告税額の）

deferred revenue　前受収益

delinquency　滞納

delinquency tax　延滞税、過怠税

delinquent　滞納している、滞納した

delinquent charge　延滞金

delinquent taxpayer　滞納者

delivery　引き渡し

delivery basis　引渡基準

departure tax　出国税

dependent agent　従属代理人

deposit　供託する

Deposit Act　供託法

deposit office　供託所

deposited article　供託物

deposited money　供託金

deposits received　預り金

depreciable asset　減価償却資産

depreciable assets tax　償却資産税

depreciation method　減価償却方法（有形減価償却資産）

depreciation period　減価償却期間（有形減価償却資産）

depreciation rate　減価償却率

derivative transaction　デリバティブ取引

descendant　卑属

design right　意匠権

designation of place for tax payment 納税地の指定

desk audit 机上調査（税務調査の一種）

determination 決定（税務当局による処分としての）

development expense [cost] 開発費

devise 遺贈

devisor 遺贈者

dilution 希薄化

dilutive effect 希薄化効果

direct foreign tax credit 直接外国税額控除

directive 通達

director 取締役、役員、理事（社団法人・財団法人の）

director's bonus 役員賞与

director's compensation [remuneration, salary] 役員給与

director's retirement allowance [benefit] 役員退職慰労金

disaffirm 取り消す

disaffirmance 取消し

disaffirmation 取消し

disallow 損金不算入とする（主に受け身で）

disallowable 損金不算入となる

discharge of delinquent tax 延滞税の免除

discharge of indebtedness 債務免除

discharge of the obligation 債務の弁済

discounted cash flow (DCF) ディスカウント・キャッシュ・フロー

discounted cash flow method DCF 法

discretion 裁量

discretionary trust 裁量信託

disguise 仮装（する）

disguise or concealment 仮装又は隠蔽

disguised accounting 仮装経理

disposal of treasury stocks 自己株式の処分

disposition 処分（行政）

disposition authority 処分行政庁

disregarded entity 課税上無視される事業体

dissolution 解散（会社の）

dissolve 解散する（会社が）

distribution of property 財産分与

distribution of residual property 残余財産の分配

dividend 配当（金）

dividend in kind 現物分配、現物配当

dividend income 配当所得

documentation 文書化

documents for identification of the individual 本人確認書類

domestic corporation [company] 内国法人

domestic law 国内法

domestic source income 国内源泉所得

domicile 居住地、住所（税務上の）

donate 寄附する、贈与する

donation 寄附金、贈与

donation contract 贈与契約

donation due to death 死因贈与

donation to foreign affiliate(s) 国外関連者に対する寄附金

donee 受贈者

dormant 休眠の

double tax(ation) relief 二重課税の排除

double taxation 二重課税

double taxation convention 租税条約

double taxation treaty 租税条約

down payment 頭金

driver's license 運転免許証

DTC → double taxation convention

DTT → double taxation treaty

dual purpose test 二重目的テスト

dual resident 二重居住者

due 期限が到来している（申告・納税の）

due date　期日（申告・納税等の）、期限（申告・納税等の）

due professional care　職業専門家が払うべき正当な注意

dummy stock　名義株

dutiable　関税が課せられる

duties　関税

duty of due care of prudent manager　善管注意義務

duty of loyalty　忠実義務

E

E&P　→ earnings and profits

EE　→ employee　**解説** 給与計算シートなどで、社会保険料の従業員負担分を示すときなどに用いられる。

E/N　→ exchange of note

earner of salary　給与所得者

earnings and profits (E&P)　税務上の利益 [米]

earnings stripping rules　過大支払利子税制（と同等の制度）

economic benefit　経済的利益

economic double taxation　経済的二重課税

economic substance　経済的実質

educational funds　教育資金

effective tax rate　（法定）実効税率

effectively connected income　ECI 所得 [米]
解説（米国から見た）非居住者・外国法人が、米国での事業に関連して稼得した所得のこと。ECI 所得に対しては事業所得として課税される。

electronic filing　電子申告

electronic service(s)　電気通信利用役務

embezzlement　横領

emigration　出国

emoloyee　従業員、使用人、被用者

Employee' Health Insurance　健康保険（従業員等の）

employee stock ownership plan (ESOP)　従業員持株制度

employee-director　使用人兼務役員

employer　雇用主、使用者

employment income　給与所得

employment income earner　給与所得者

end of accounting period　期末

ending balance　期末残高

endorsement　裏書

endorser　裏書人

endowment　寄附行為

enforcement　施行（法令の）、執行（行政行為の）

enroll　加入する（年金制度に）

enter　登録する

enterprise tax　事業税

entertainment expense [cost]　交際費

entire income approach [principle]　総合主義

entity　事業体

entity transparent for tax purposes　課税上透明体

entrepreneur　企業家

entrepreneur risk　企業家リスク

entrustee　受託者

entry　登録

equipment　器具

ER　→employer　**解説** 給与計算シートなどで、社会保険料の会社負担分を示すときなどに用いられる。

ESOP　→ employee stock ownership plan

estate tax　相続税

estimate　推計

estimated tax prepayment　予定納税

estimated useful life　見積り耐用年数

ex ante　事前の

ex post　事後の

examine　調査する

excess credit limit　控除余裕額（外国税額控除制度の）

excess foreign tax　控除限度超過額（外国税額控除制度の）

excessive depreciation expenses　減価償却超過額

exchange of note (E/N)　交換公文（租税条約を含む条約の）

exclude　除外する（益金から）

exclude from deductible expense　損金不算入とする

excluding tax　税抜き（で、の）

exclusion from deductible expense　損金不算入

exclusion from gross profit　益金不算入

exempt　免除する、免除された

exempted　免除された

exemption　免除

exemption for spouses　配偶者控除

exemption method　国外所得免除方式　cf. tax credit method

exemption of fixed assets tax　固定資産税の免除

exit tax　出国税

exit tax system　外国転出時所得課税制度

expat　→ expatriate

expatriate　非居住外国人、外国駐在員

expatriation tax　出国税（米国）

expense　費用

expense of contribution or donation　寄附金

expenses related to household　家事関連費

expiration　終了（有効期限などの）

expiration date　失効日

expire　期間が終わる

expropriate　収用する

expropriation　収用

extend　延長する

extension　延長

extension of tax (return) filing deadline　申告期限の延長

extension of tax payment due date　納期限の延長

extension of time to file tax return　申告期限の延長

extension of time to pay tax　納期限の延長

extension to ～　～への延長

extinguish of payment obligation　支払義務の消滅（源泉徴収の契機となるタイミングとしての）

E
F

F

factual analysis　事実分析

fail to　～に失敗する、～が漏れる、～できない

failure to　～に失敗した、～が漏れた、～できない

family company　同族会社

family register　戸籍

FATCA　→ Foreign Account Tax Compliance Act

FDAP Income　→ Fixed, Determinable, Annual, Periodical Income [米]

federal (income) tax　連邦税

fiduciary　受託者（信託における。trustee より広い概念）

field audit　実地調査

field tax audit　臨場［実地］税務調査

file　提出する

filing　提出

filing deadline　提出期限

filing due date　提出期限

filing extention　提出期限の延長

final tax　確定税額

final tax return　確定申告書

finance lease with transfer of ownership　所有権移転ファイナンスリース

finance lease without transfer of ownership　所有権移転外ファイナンスリース

financial closing　決算（会計の）

financial year (FY)　会計年度、事業年度

fine　罰金

fire insurance　火災保険

fire insurance premium　火災保険料

fiscal year (FY)　事業年度

fiscally transparent entity　課税上透明体

fixed amount deduction　定額控除

fixed asset register　固定資産台帳

fixed asset(s) tax　固定資産税

fixed cost　固定費

fixed place of business　固定的な事業の場所

Fixed, Determinable, Annual, or Periodical (FDAP) Income　FDAP 所得

fixture　器具、備品

flow-through　フロースルー（＝パススルー）の（和英見出し参照）

flow-through entity　フロースルー（＝パススルー）事業体（和英見出し参照）

flow-through taxation　構成員課税
解説 フロースルー（＝パススルー）事業体の構成員に直接税を課すこと。

for tax purpose(s)　税務上の、税（法）の見地からすると

force majeure　不可抗力

force of attraction　吸引力

Foreign Account Tax Compliance Act (FATCA)　外国口座税務コンプライアンス法 米

foreign corporation [company]　外国法人

foreign currency transaction　外貨建取引

foreign currency translation　外貨換算

foreign dividend　外国配当

foreign dividend exepmtion system　外国子会社配当益金不算入制度

foreign exchange rate　外国為替相場

foreign income tax　外国所得税

foreign investment trust　外国投資信託

foreign related company/foreign affiliate(d) company　国外関連者

foreign source(d) income　国外源泉所得

foreign tax credit (FTC)　外国税額控除

foreign tax withheld at source　外国源泉税

foreign withholding tax　外国源泉税

forfait　見積課税制度（小規模事業者に簡便な税額計算を認める簡易課税制度）

for-profit corporation　営利法人

forward (exchange) rate　予約レート（為替）

forward rate　先物レート（為替）

401k plan [401(k) plan]　内国歳入法 401 条（K 項）を根拠とする税制適格年金制度（米国の確定拠出年金制度の 1 つ）

franchise tax　事業税（米国の州税。所得を課税標準としないものもある）

free rent　フリーレント

fringe benefit　経済的利益

frivolus (tax) position　意図的に過大申告をして還付加算金の受領を企図する行為。こうした行為に追加ペナルティを課す国もある。

FTC　→ foreign tax credit

full cost　総費用

functional analysis　機能分析

functional and factual analysis　機能事実分析

furnishment　備品

furniture　備品

FY　→ financial year、fiscal year

G

gain on disposal of ～　～処分益

gain on sale of ～　～売却益

gazette　官報

general administrative expenses　一般管理費

general incorporated association　一般社団法人

general incorporated foundation　一般財団法人

general ledger　総勘定元帳

general partner　無限責任社員

general provision for bad debt　貸倒引当金（一般評価金銭債権に係る）

general shareholder meeting　定時株主総会

gift　贈与

gift during life　生前贈与

gift profit　受贈益

gift tax　贈与税

GILTI　→ Global Intangible Low-Taxed Income

GK　→ Goudou Kaisha

Global Anti-Base Erosion Proposal (GLoBE)　税源浸食への対抗措置

Global Intangible Low-Taxed Income (GILTI)　軽課税無形資産所得（米国の税制度の一つ）

GloBE　→ Global Anti-Base Erosion Proposal

golf club membership　ゴルフ会員権

good faith　善意（法律）

goods in process　仕掛品

goodwill　営業権、のれん

Goudou Kaisha (GK)　合同会社

government bonds　国債

government grant [subsidy]　国庫補助金

grace period　猶予期間

graduated tax rates　累進税率

graduated taxation　累進課税

grant　①許可（する）、②（政府等からの）補助金、助成金、

green card　永住者カード（グリーンカード）
解説 米国の永住権の資格を証明するカード。

gross average method　総平均法

gross income　総収入

gross negligence　重過失

gross profit　売上総利益、粗利（益）、益金

gross up　グロスアップ

gross up computation　グロスアップ計算

group orgaisation chart　資本関係図

group taxation regime　グループ法人税制

H

hair at law　法定相続人

head office　本店、本社

headquarters (HQ)　本店、本社

head-to-maturity bond　満期保有目的債券

health (care) insurance　健康保険

heavy additional charge　重加算金

heavy additional tax　重加算税

heavy penalty tax　重加算税

heir　相続人

higher-than-standard tax rate　超過税率

hire purchase　分割払い（主に英国）

historical cost　取得原価

home company　出向元法人

host company　出向先法人

household expenses　家事費

housing allowance　住宅手当

HQ　→ headquarters

hybrid entity　ハイブリッド事業体

hypo-tax　→ hypothetical tax

hypothetical tax　みなし税（金）、ハイポタックス

I

IGS　→ inter-group services

IIR　→ income inclusion rule

illegal income　不法所得

immediate　直前の

immediately　直前に

immovable property　不動産

impose　課す（税金などを）

imposition　賦課

improvement expense　改良費

imputed income　帰属所得

in arrears　滞納している

in bad faith　悪意の（法律）

in good faith　善意の（法律）

incidental cost　付随費用

include　益金算入とする

including tax　税込み（で、の）

inclusion　益金算入

income inclusion rule (IIR)　所得合算ルール

income splitting method　二分二乗方式、所得分割法

income tax　所得（に対する）税　注　外国では日本の法人税と所得税が同じ法律において規定されていることがよくある。このため、文脈に応じ、法人に対するものを指すこともあるので注意。

income tax basis　課税標準

income tax credit　所得税額控除

income tax withheld at source　源泉所得税

indefinitely　制限無く、無制限に

indemnify　賠償する、（法律上）保護する

independent agent　独立代理人

indirect foreign tax credit　間接外国税額控除　注　日本の現行法には間接外国税額控除制度は存在しない

indirect shareholding　間接保有（株式等の）

indirect tax　間接税

individual income tax　個人所得税

individual income tax return　個人所得税の申告書

industrial property right　工業所有権

information return　情報申告

inheritance　相続

inheritance of bequest　遺産相続

inheritance tax　相続税

input consumption tax　仮払消費税等

input VAT　仮払 VAT　解説　外国の付加価値税制に基づき支払った付加価値税の額。日本の仮払消費税に類似したもの。

inspection　検収

instalment　分割払い

instalment plan　分割払い（主に米国）

insurance　保険

insurance contract　保険契約

insurance money　保険金

insurance policy　保険証券

insurance premium　保険料

intangible asset　無形資産

intangible fixed asset　無形固定資産

intangible property (IP)　無形資産

intangibles　無形資産

interco　→ intercomapany

intercompany　グループ会社間の

interest　利子

interest charge　延滞税（期限後申告による税の利子）

interest income　受取利子、利子所得

interest on refund of tax　還付加算金

interest paid　支払利子

interest received　受取利子、受取利息

interest tax　利子税

interest-free loan　無利息貸付け

inter-group services (IGS)　グループ間役務提供

interim (tax) return　中間申告、中間申告書

interim payment　中間納付

internal dealing　内部取引（本支店間及び支店間の取引）

internal transaction　内部取引（本支店間及び支店間の取引又は同一法人内部の原価計算や減価償却等）

international double taxation　国際的二重課税

international tax (taxation)　国際課税

interpretation based on economic reality　経済的観察法

interquartile　四分位値の範囲内

interquartile range　四分位幅［レンジ］

interruption of statute of limitations　時効の中断

interset　持分

intestate　遺言をしていない

invalidate　取り消す

inventory at the beginning of the period　期首商品棚卸高

inventory at the end of the period　期末商品棚卸高

inventory of property　財産目録（清算会社の）

investigation　税務調査

investment trust　投資信託

IP　→ intangible property

issued capital　資本金

issued share capital　資本金

itemised statement of account　勘定科目内訳明細書

J

Japan source income　日本国内源泉所得

Japanese municipal bonds　地方債

joint tenancy　合有不動産権（米国における財産の保有形態。二以上の者による不動産の共有。相続時の手続きが通常と異なる）

joint trust　合同運用信託

journal　仕訳（日記）帳

journal entry　仕訳（の入力）

journal slip　仕訳伝票

judgement　判決

judicial　司法上の、裁判の

judicial double taxation　法的二重課税

judicial power　司法権

judicial precedent　判例

judicial scrivener　司法書士

juridical　司法上の、法律上の、法律的な

jurisdiction　司法権（の及ぶ範囲）、法域

K

Kabushiki Kaisha (KK)　株式会社

keepwell agreement　キープウェル契約

keepwell letter　経営指導念書

key money　権利金、敷金

KK　→ Kabushiki Kaish

know how　ノウハウ

L

labour insurance　労働保険

large corporation　大法人

last in, first out method (LIFO)　後入先出法

late filing　期限後申告

late filing charge　無申告加算税、無申告加算金

late payment charge (for withholding tax)　不納付加算税

late payment penalty　加算税

law　法、法律

laws and ordinances　法令

lawsuit　訴訟

LC　→ letter of credit

lease　リース、賃貸、賃借

lease agreement [contract]　リース契約（書）、賃貸借契約（書）

lease deposit　敷金

lease obligation　リース債務

leasehold (right)　借地権

leasehold improvement　建物附属設備（賃借物件改良費用）

ledger　元帳

legal　法的な、合法的な

legal capital reserve　資本準備金

legal form　法（的）形式、法（的）形態

legal hair　法定相続人

legal opinion　法律意見

legal person　法人

legal procedure　法的手続、訴訟手続

legal requirement　法的要件

legal reserve　法定準備金

legal retained earnings　利益準備金

legal share of legacy　法定相続分

legal successor　法定相続人

legal title　法的所有権

legal welfare cost [expense]　法定福利費

legally　法的に

legatee　遺産受取人

legislation　法律、立法

legislative　法律上の、立法上の

legitimate child　嫡出子

lender　貸手

less　より少ない

less than　未満

lessee　リースの借手

lessor　リースの貸手

letter of credit (LC)　信用状

letter of engagement　業務委託契約書

letter ruling　文書回答（税務当局の）

levy　徴収する、（税などを）課する、課徴金、税金　例 per capita levy（法人住民税・個人住民税の均等割）

life insurance　生命保険

life insurance premium　生命保険料

LIFO → last in, first out method

limit 限度、制限する

limitation 限度

limitation of actions 出訴期間

limitation on benefits (LOB) provision 特典制限条項

limited liability company (LLC) 有限責任会社

limited liability partnership (LLP) 有限責任組合

limited partner (LP) 有限責任社員

limited partnership (LPS) 有限責任組合

limited risk distributor リスク限定販売会社

lineal ascendant 直系尊属

liquidate 清算する（会社を）

liquidating corporation 清算中の法人

liquidation 清算（会社の）

liquidation dividend [distribution] 清算配当

liquidator 清算人

listed company 上場企業

listed stock 上場株式

litigation 訴訟

LLC → limited liability company

LLP → limited liability partnership

loan 貸付金、借入金

loan for consumption 消費貸借

loan for use 使用貸借

loan receivables 貸付金債権

LOB provision → limitation on benefits provision

local file ローカルファイル

local government 地方自治体

location of property 財産の所在

location saving ロケーションセービング（和英見出し参照）

long-term debt in foreign currency 長期外貨建債務

long-term loan payable 長期借入金

long-term receivable in foreign currency 長期外貨建債権

long-term suspended claims 長期棚上債権

loss 損失

loss for ～における損失

loss from ～から生じた損失

loss on ～に係る（～生じた）損失

losses carried forward 繰越欠損金

low tax jurisdiction 低税率国［地域］、軽課税国［地域］

low value-adding intra-group services 低付加価値のグループ間役務提供

lower of cost and net realisable value 低価法

LP → limited partner

LPS → limited parnership

lump-sum 一括の

lump-sum payment 一括払い

L

M

M

machinery and equipment 機械装置

make adjustment of final return 申告調整する

mala fides 悪意（法律）

management fee 経営指導料、マネジメントフィー

managing director 代表取締役

manufacturing cost 製造原価

MAP → mutual agreement procedure

margin 利ざや、マージン

marine procedure commission agent　海事代理士

marketing intangible　マーケティング無形資産

mark-up　利益の上乗せ部分、マークアップ

master file　マスターファイル

material　資料

materialise　実現する（リスクなどが）

maturity date　満期日

maximum amount of depreciation　償却限度額

mean　平均

median　中央値

medical care insurance premium　介護保険料

medical check-up　健康診断

medical expense　医療費

medical expense deduction　医療費控除

meeting minutes　議事録

member　社員（社団法人・財団法人の）

member of board of directors　取締役

memorandum　覚書

memorandum of association　定款

memorandum value　備忘価額

merge　合併する

merged company　消滅会社（合併による）

merger　合併

method of taxation on bequest　遺産税方式

method of taxation on legatee　遺産取得税方式

method of translation at historical rate　取得時換算法

minimum standard　最低基準

minimum tax　ミニマムタックス（和英見出し参照）

Ministry of Finance　財務省

minutes of board of directors' meeting　取締役会議事録

minutes of shareholders' meeting　株主総会議事録

misc　→ miscellaneous

miscellaneous　雑多な

miscellaneous expense　雑費

miscellaneous income　雑収入、雑所得

miscellaneous loss　雑損失

MLI　→ Multilateral Instrument

MNE　→ multinational enterprise

model tax convention　モデル租税条約

MOF　→ Ministry of Finance

money in bank account　預貯金

money laundering　マネーロンダリング

money paid into court　供託金

monthly　月次の、毎月の

more than　を超える、超

mortgage　抵当権、譲渡担保

motor vehicle tax　自動車税

mould　金型

movable property　動産

moving average　移動平均

moving average method　移動平均法

Multilateral Convention to Implement Tax Treaty Related Measures to Prevent Base Erosion and Profit Shifting　BEPS防止措置実施条約（＝MLI）

Multilateral Instrument (MLI)　BEPS防止措置実施条約

multinational enterprise (MNE)　多国籍企業

municipal　市町村の

municipal ordinance　条例（市町村の）

municipality　市、町、村

muniment of title　権利証

mutual agreement procedure (MAP)　相互協議

N

N/A → not applicable

national tax 国税

National Tax Agency (NTA) 国税庁（日本の）

nationality 国籍

natural person 自然人

negligence 過失

net income 当期純利益

net loss 欠損金、純損失

net loss carry back 欠損金の繰戻還付

net loss carryforward 繰越欠損金

net of income tax 税引き後

net of tax(es) 税引き後

net operating loss (NOL) 欠損金

next period 翌期、来期

next taxable period 翌課税期間（消費税等の）

nexus ネクサス（和英見出し参照）

night-duty allowance 夜勤手当

Nin-i Kumiai (NK) 任意組合

NK → Nin-i Kumiai

NOL → net operating loss

nominal tax rate 表面税率

non tax-qualified 税制非適格の

non-cancellable lease 解約不能のリース

non-current liability 固定負債

non-deductible 損金不算入の

non-default 法定のものでない

non-discrimination provision 無差別条項

non-life insurance 損害保険

non-operating asset 遊休資産

non-operating expense 営業外費用

non-operating profit 営業外収益

non-ownership-transfer finance lease 所有権移転外ファイナンスリース

non-penal fine 過料

non-permanent resident 非永住者

non-qualified 非適格の

non-qualified stock option 税制非適格ストックオプション

non-resident 非居住者

non-resident alien 非居住外国人

non-routine transaction 非経常取引

non-taxable 非課税の

non-taxable assets 非課税財産

non-taxable income 非課税所得

non-taxable sales 非課税売上

non-taxable transaction 非課税取引

no-par (value) share [stock] 無額面株式

not applicable (N/A) 該当無し

note receivable 受取手形

notice of assessment 賦課決定通知書

notice of correction 更正通知書

notification 届出、通知書

notification of tax payment 納税の告知

NTA → National Tax Agency

O

object of taxation 課税物件

obligation to pay tax 納税義務

obligation to withhold tax 源泉徴収義務

obsolete 陳腐化した

occupation　占有

occupy　占有する

OECD　→ Organisation of Economic Cooperation and Development

OECD Model Tax Convention (on Income and on Capital)　OECD モデル租税条約

OECD Transfer Pricing Guidelines for Multinational Enterprises and Tax Administrations　OECD 移転価格ガイドライン

office audit　机上調査

official assessment system　賦課課税制度

official discount rate　公定歩合

offset　相殺

old stock　旧株

on or after　以降

on or before　以前

on-call services　オンコールサービス（和英見出し参照）

on-time return　期限内申告

183-day rule　183 日ルール

onus of proof　立証責任

open　税務調査未済の

opening balance　期首残高

operating loss　営業損失

operating margin　営業利益率

operating profit　営業利益

operating revenue　営業収入

option　選択（できること）

optional　任意の、自由選択の

or less　以下

or more　以上

ordinance　条例、法令

ordinary account　普通預金

ordinary depreciation　普通償却

ordinary loss　経常損失

ordinary profit　経常利益

ordinary share [stock]　普通株式

Organisation of Economy and Commercial Development (OECD)　経済協力開発機構

other capital surplus　その他資本剰余金

output VAT　仮受 VAT　解説 外国の付加価値税制に基づき受領した付加価値税の額。日本の仮受消費税に類似したもの。

outstanding　未払いの、(株式等が) 発行済の

outstanding　発行済の

outstanding shares [stocks]　発行済株式

overdraft　当座貸越、当座借越

overdue　延滞した、期限を過ぎた

overdue tax return　期限後申告

overhead cost　間接経費

overhead expense　間接経費

overpaid　過払いの

overpayment　過大納付

overseas transaction　海外取引

overseas travel expense　海外渡航費

overtime　残業

overtime allowance　残業手当

own share　自己株式

ownership　所有権

ownership-transfer finance lease　所有権移転ファイナンスリース

P

paid leave　有給休暇

paid-in capital　資本金（払込資本）

paper company　ペーパーカンパニー

par value　額面金額（株式等の）

par value share 額面株式

par value stock 額面株式

parent company 親会社

partition of bequest 遺産分割

partner パートナー（組合の）

partnership 組合、パートナーシップ

partnership interest 組合の持分

party 関係者、当事者

passive income 受動（的）所得、資産性所得

pass-through パススルーの（和英見出し参照）

pass-through businesses（主に複数形で用いる） パススルー事業体（和英見出し参照）

pass-through entity パススルー事業体（和英見出し参照）

pass-through taxation 構成員課税

past due 期限後の、延滞している

past due return 期限後申告書

patent (right) 特許権

patent attorney 弁理士

patent box パテントボックス（和英見出し参照）

pay money into court 供託する（お金を）

pay slip 給与明細

pay stub 給与明細

payable 未払いの

pay-as-you-earn (PAYE) 主に給与に係る源泉所得課税方式

PAYE → pay-as-you-earn

payment 納付（税金などの）

payment by beneficiary 工事負担金

payment deadline 納付期限

payment due 納付期限

payment due date 納付期限

payment extension 納期限の延長

payment in kind 現物給付、現物給与

payment of retirement allowance due to termination 退職金の打切り支給

payment of tax in kind 物納

payment record 支払調書

payroll 賃金台帳

payroll book 賃金台帳

payroll table 給与テーブル

payroll tax 給与税

payslip 給与明細、給与支払報告書

PE → permanent establishment

penalty 加算税

penalty charge 罰金

penalty tax 加算税

pending case 係属中の訴訟事案

pending lawsuit 係属中の訴訟事案

pension 年金

pension fund 年金基金

pension plan 年金制度

pension scheme 年金制度

pensioner 年金受給者

per capita 一人当たり

per diem 日当

per se それ自体で

per se corporation per se 法人 解説 米国税法上法人として扱われる事業体のこと。

percentage of completion method 工事進行基準

performance-based compensation 業績連動給与

periodical accounting of profit and loss 期間損益計算

periodical deposits 定期積金

permanent establishment (PE) 恒久的施設

permanent resident 永住者

person in charge 担当者

person who renounced inheritance 相続を放棄した者

personal income tax　個人所得税

personal income tax return　個人所得税の申告書

personal service　人的役務

personnel　人員

petition　嘆願（書）、嘆願する

phantom stock　ファントムストック（和英見出し参照）

physical inspection　実査

physical inventory count　実地棚卸

Pillar 1 [one]　第一の柱

Pillar 2 [two]　第二の柱

place for tax payment　納税地

place of central management and control　管理支配地（基準）

place of management　事業の管理の場所

place of tax payment　納税地

PLI　→ profit level indicator

PO　→ purchase order

policyholder dividends　契約者配当

positive assets　積極財産

post tax　税引き後

postponement　猶予

postponement of collection　徴収猶予

postponement of tax payment　延納

power　委任（された権限）

power of attorney　委任状

P

predecessor corporation　被合併法人

pre-existing　既存の

prefectural ordinance　条例（都道府県の）

prefectural tax　道府県民税

prefectural tax office　道府県税事務所

preferential tax treatment　優遇税制

preferred share [stock]　優先株式

premises　建物（土地や付属物も含まれる）

premium　権利金

pre-operating cost　開業費

prepaid expense　前払費用

preparation　作成（書類の）

preparatory activity　準備的活動

prepare　作成する（書類を）

prepayment　予納

preservation clause　プリザベーション条項（和英見出し参照）

presumptive assessment　推計課税

previous year　前年

previous　～の前の　例 previous fiscal year　前事業年度

price adjustment　価格調整

price adjustment clause　価格調整条項

principal　本人（代理人との関係で）、（貸付金等の）元本

principal purpose test　主要目的テスト

principal tax　本税

principle of estoppel　禁反言の法理

principle of legality of taxation　租税法律主義

principle of taxation on beneficial owner　実質（所得者）課税の原則

private company　非公開会社

private ruling　プライベートルーリング（和英見出し参照）

pro rata　比例して、プロラタ

probate　（遺言の）検認、プロベート（[米] 裁判所の管轄下で行われる遺産分割、相続の手続き）

procedure for collection of delinquent tax　滞納処分

proceedings　法的手続、訴訟手続

processing cost　加工費

profit and loss transaction　損益取引

profit attributable to permanent establishment (PE)　恒久的施設（PE）帰属所得

profit corporation　営利法人

profit from redemption of discount bonds 割引債の償還差益

profit from trust 信託利益

profit level indicator 利益水準指標

profit on redemption amount of discount bonds 割引債の償還金

profit reserve 利益積立金額

profit split method 利益分割法

profit-making business 収益事業

profits of an enterprise 企業の利得

pro-forma taxation 外形標準課税

progression 累進課税

progressive tax rates 累進税率

promissory note 約束手形、融資契約書、借用証書

promulgation 公布

property 財産

property prohibited from seizure 差押禁止財産

property status survey 財産状況の調査（会社の清算における）

property tax 固定資産税

proprietor 事業主

protocol 議定書

provision (for ~) 引当金 例 provision for bad debt 貸倒引当金

provision of electronic service(s) 電気通信利用役務の提供

provision of personal service(s) 人的役務の提供

provision of service(s) 役務提供

provisional 仮の、暫定的な、臨時の

provisional disposition 仮処分

provisional execution 仮執行

provisional financial closing 仮決算

provisional registration 仮登記

provisional seizure 仮差押

provisional tax payment 予定納税

prudent man rule 善管注意義務

PSM → profit split method

public auction 公売

public charges 公課

public company 公開会社

public interest incorporated association 公益社団法人

public interest incorporated foundation 公益財団法人

public notification 公示

public pension 公的年金

public pension, etc. 公的年金等

purchase order 注文書

purchase tax credit 仕入税額控除

Q

qualified 税制適格の

qualified corporate reorganisation 適格組織再編成

qualifying conditions for tax purposes 税制適格要件

quartile 四分位

quartile analysis 四分位分析

questionnaire 質問書

R

ratio of operating profit to total costs 総費用営業利益率

real estate 不動産

real estate appraiser 不動産鑑定士

real estate income 不動産所得

real property 不動産

real property acquisition tax 不動産取得税

realisation principle 実現主義

reassess 更正する

reassessment 更正

reassessment notice 更正通知書

rebate on sales 売上割戻し

receipt 領収書、受領

receivable in foreign currency 外貨建債権

reception stamp 受付印

reciprocal 相互主義の

reciprocity 相互主義

recognise 認識する

recognition 認識

record 登録、登録する

recordation 登録（権利などの）

recovery of tax 還付（税金の）

recuperation 療養

redeem 償還する、買い戻す（自己株式を）

redemption 償還、買戻し

redemption of treasury stock 自己株式の取得（買い戻し）

reduced tax rate 軽減税率

reducing balance method 定率法（減価償却の）

reduction in capital 減資

reduction of fixed assets tax 固定資産税の減額

refund 還付する（税金を）

refund of tax 還付（税金の）

register 登記する、登録する

registered capital 授権資本

registered seal 実印

registrar 登記官

registration 登記、登録

registration and license tax 登録免許税

registration duty 登録免許税

regulation 規制、法規

related company [corporation] 関連会社

related party 関連者

related party transaction 国外関連取引、関連者間取引

relative 親族

relative by affinity 姻族

release of seizure 差押の解除

relevant 関連する、適切な

relief 軽減、免除

relieve 軽減する、免除する

remaining useful life 残存耐用年数

remarkably low value 著しく低い価額

remuneration 報酬

renewal 更新（契約などの）

renewal fee [charge] 更新料

rent 賃借料、賃貸料

rental expense 支払賃借料

rental income 賃貸料収入

rent-free フリーレントの

repair expense [cost] 修繕費

repay 返還する（収入した補助金などを）

repayment 返還（収入した補助金などの）

repayment of capital 資本の払戻し

replacement of business property 事業用資産の買換え

representative 代表者（法人の）

representative director 代表取締役

representative office 駐在員事務所

representative's seal 代表者印

request for reconsideration 審査請求

request for reexamination 再調査の請求

resale price 再販売価格

resale price method 再販売価格基準法

rescind 取り消す

research and development expense 試験研究費

residence 居所

residency certificate 居住者証明書

resident 居住者

residential property 居住用財産

residual profit split method 残余利益分割法

residual property 残余財産

resignation 退職

resolution 決議

resolution date 決議の日

respectively それぞれに

restricted stock（RS） 譲渡制限株式、リストリクテッドストック

restricted stock unit（RSU） リストリクテッドストックユニット

restriction on share transfer 株式譲渡制限

retail method 売価還元法

retained earnings 利益剰余金

retained earnings reserve 利益準備金

retire 退職する

retirement 退職

retirement 退職、除却（固定資産の）

retirement allowance 退職金、退職手当金

retirement allowance policy 退職給与規定

retirement benefit 退職金

retirement income 退職所得

retirement of stock 株式の消却

retirement of treasury shares 自己株式の消却

retirement pension 退職年金

returned goods 返品

revenue 収益

revenue expenditure 収益的支出

revenue expense 収益的支出

revenue recognition standard 収益(の)認識基準

revenue recognition 収益認識

revenue stamp 収入印紙

reversal method 洗替法

reversal of taxation 課税処分の取消し

reverse charge mechanism リバースチャージ方式

reverse stock split 株式併合

revocation 取消し

revokable trust 撤回可能生前信託

revoke 取り消す

right of indemnity 求償権

right of lease 賃借権

right of survivorship 生存者取得権

right of use 使用権

right on land 土地の上に存する権利

risk リスク、危険

robbery 盗難

rollback ロールバック（和英見出し参照）

rounding off 端数切り捨て

routine profit 基本的利益

royalty 使用料、ロイヤルティ

RS → restricted stock

RSU → restricted stock unit

rules of employment　就業規則

rules on segregation of duties　職務分掌規程

ruling　通達（行政庁による）、判示

S

safe harbour rule　セーフハーバールール（和英見出し参照）

salary (payment) slip　給与明細、給与支払報告書

salary in kind　現物給与

salary income　給与所得

sale and lease back transaction　セールアンドリースバック（和英見出し参照）

sales basis　販売基準

sales discount　売上値引

sales rebate　売上割戻し

saving clause　セービング条項（和英見出し参照）

schedule　明細

scholarships　奨学金

seal　印章、押印

seal impression　印鑑（印影）

second　出向させる　例 second personnel to an overseas subsidiary（海外子会社に社員を出向させる）

seconded employee [personnel]　出向者

secondee　出向者

secondment　出向

secondment agreement　出向契約

secret comparable　シークレット・コンパラブル（和英見出し参照）

sectional accounting　区分経理

sectional ownership　区分所有権

securities　有価証券

securities held for trading　売買目的有価証券

security　担保

security deposit　敷金、保証金

segmented profit or loss　セグメント損益（和英見出し参照）

segregation of duties　職務分掌

seizure　差押

self assessment　申告納税

self assessment system　申告納税方式

self-assessed income tax　申告所得税

self-consumption　自家消費

self-enforcement　自力執行権（税務官庁の）

selling expenses　販売費

selling, general and administrative expenses　販売費及び一般管理費

separate assessment　分離課税

separate assessment system　分離課税方式

separate self-assessment taxation　申告分離課税

separate withholding taxation at source　源泉分離課税

service　送達

service PE　サービス PE（和英見出し参照）

service provided [rendered]　提供を受けた役務

service provision　役務提供

settlement　清算、和解

settlement agreement　和解契約

settlement fee　清算費用

settlement procedures　清算手続

settlor　委託者（信託の）

sham transaction　仮装取引

share　株式

share capital　株主からの払込金額のうち株式の額面金額に相当する部分の金額

share consideration 株式対価
share consolidation 株式併合
share dividend 株式配当
share for share exchange 株式交換
share issuance 株式発行
share premium 資本剰余金
share redemption 株式償還、減資
share repurchase 自己株式の購入
share-based compensation 株式報酬
share-based compensation expense 株式報酬費用
shareholder 株主
shareholders' meeting 株主総会
share-issuing expense 新株発行費
shell company ペーパーカンパニー、休眠会社
shipping 出荷
shipping basis 出荷基準、発送基準
shipping standard 出荷基準
short depreciation 減価償却不足額
shortcut method 簡便法
short-term debt in foreign currency 短期外貨建債務
short-term receivable in foreign currency 短期外貨建債権
signature 自署
sister company 兄弟会社
site 場所
situs 所在地
size-based taxation 外形標準課税
sleeping partnership 匿名組合
small and medium (-sized) enterprise (SME) 中小法人、中小企業者等
small-scale enterprise 小規模事業者
SME → small and medium (-sized) enterprise
social expenses 交際費
social insurance 社会保険
social insurance labor consultant 社会保険労務士
social insurance premium 社会保険料
social insurance system 社会保険制度
social insurance tax 社会保険税
social security agreement 社会保障協定
social security number 社会保障番号
sole proprietorship 個人事業主
source of income 所得源泉
source rule ソースルール（和英見出し参照）
sovereign of taxation 課税主体
SPC → special purpose company
special contribution 特別の寄与
special deduction 特別控除
special depreciation 特別償却
special exemption for spouses 配偶者特別控除
special liquidation 特別清算
special purpose company (SPC) 特別目的会社
specific account 特定口座（株式等の）
specific identification method 個別法（棚卸資産の評価方法）
specified beneficiary securities issuing trust 特定受益証券発行信託
spin-off 会社分割
spot (exchange) rate 直物レート、現物相場
spot transaction 現物取引
spouse 配偶者
staff training expense 教育訓練費
stage of completion of contracted activity 進捗度（工事進行基準における）
stamp duty 印紙税
standard 基準、標準
standard cost 標準原価
standard tax rate 標準税率
start-up company 開業後間もない会社

S

start-up cost (expense) 開業費

state (income) tax 州税 米

stated value 額面金額（株式等の）

statement of changes in shareholders' equity 株主資本等変動計算書

status of residence 在留資格

statute 法令

statutory 法定の

statutory depreciation 法定償却

statutory due date for tax payment 法定納期限

statutory interest 法定利息

statutory reserve 法定準備金

statutory reserved portion 遺留分

statutory tax rate 法定税率

statutory useful life 法定耐用年数

stipulate 規定する

stock 株式、在庫

stock buyback 自己株式の購入

stock consideration 株式対価

stock consolidation 株式併合

stock dividend 株式配当

stock issuance cost 株式交付費

stock option ストックオプション

stock redemption 株式償還、減資

stock split 株式分割

stock without quotation 取引相場のない株式

stock-based compensation 株式報酬

stock-based compensation expense 株式報酬費用

straight line method 均等償却、定額法（減価償却方法）

structure 構築物、構造

STTR → subject to tax rule

subcontract cost 外注（加工）費

subject to ～の対象となる（課税などの）

subject to tax rule (STTR) 租税条約の特典否認ルール

submission 提出

submit 提出する

subscription for stock 株式の引受け

subsequent ～に続く、後続の

substance over form doctrine 実質主義 解説 法律上の外観より経済的な実質を重視するという考え方。

substantial 実質的な、重要な

substantially 実質的に

subtract 減算する

subtraction 減算

succeed 引き継ぐ

succession 承継、引き継ぎ

succession per stirp(e)s 代襲相続

successive inheritance 相次相続

successor 承継人、承継法人

successor per stirp(e)s 代襲相続人

suffice 満たす、十分である

sufficient 十分な

summary statement of business 事業概況説明書

super royalty provision スーパーロイヤルティ条項（和英見出し参照）

supporting evidence 根拠証憑

supporting material 根拠資料

Supreme Court 最高裁判所

surcharge 付加税 解説 本来の税に上乗せで加算される追加的な税のこと。

surface right 地上権

surplus 剰余金

surtax 付加税 解説 本来の税に上乗せで加算される追加的な税のこと。

suspension of seizure 差押の猶予

suspension of statute of limitations 時効の停止

S

T

tangible fixed asset　有形固定資産

tariff　関税

tariff rate　関税率

tariff schedule　実行関税率表

tariff table　関税率表

tax　税（金）

tax agent　納税管理人

tax amount　税額

tax appeal　不服申立

tax assessment notice　課税明細書（賦課決定方式における）

tax audit　税務調査、任意調査

tax audit on a voluntary basis　任意調査

tax auditor　税務調査官

tax authorities　税務当局

tax avoidance　租税回避

tax calculation　税金の計算

tax case　税務訴訟

tax code　税法

tax compliance　税に関する法令の遵守、コンプライアンス業務（税務・会計の文脈において、特に企業の記帳及び申告納税業務をこのように称することがある）

tax compliance service　税務申告等の税に関する法令遵守のための業務を行うサービス

tax computation　税金の計算

tax concession　税制上の優遇措置

tax consolidation　連結納税

tax consolidation system　連結納税制度

tax consultation　税務相談

tax convention　租税条約

tax court　租税裁判所

tax credit　税額控除

tax credit method　（外国）税額控除方式

tax declaration　税務申告

tax deductible　損金に算入できる

tax deferral measure　課税の繰延べ措置

tax delinquency　滞納（税金の）

tax due　納税額

tax equalisation　タックスイコライゼーション（和英見出し参照）

tax evader　脱税者

tax evasion　脱税

tax examination　税務調査

tax examiner　税務調査官

tax exclusive　税抜き（で、の）

tax exemption　非課税

tax filing　税金の申告

tax form　税務の申告書

tax free　税金が課されない、非課税の

tax haven　タックスヘイブン

tax holiday　タックスホリデー

tax incentive　税制上の優遇措置

tax inclusive　税込み（で、の）

tax information exchange agreement　税に関する情報交換協定

tax investigation　税務調査

tax jurisdiction　税務上の管轄地域

tax law　租税法

tax liability　納付すべき税額、税金を納付すべき義務、納税義務、未納税金、租税債務

tax loss　欠損金（税務上）

tax loss carryback　欠損金の繰戻し

tax loss carryforward　欠損金の繰越し

tax losses brought forward　繰越欠損金（税務上）

tax losses carried forward　繰越欠損金（税務上）

tax notice　納付告知書

tax notice (of assessment)　賦課決定通知書（固定資産税などの）

tax obligation　納税義務

tax office　税務署

tax payment slip　納付書

tax proxy　税務代理

tax rate　税率

tax reassessment　更正処分

tax reassessment notice　更正通知書

tax reform　税制改正

tax reform bill　税制改正法案

tax refund　税金の還付

tax regime　税制

tax return　税務申告書

tax return filed by the due date　期限内申告書

tax return preparation　申告書の作成

tax saving　節税

tax sparing credit　タックス・スペアリング・クレジット（和英見出し参照）、みなし外国税額控除

tax system　税制

tax threshold　課税最低限

tax treaty　租税条約

taxable　課税の対象となる

taxable basis　課税標準

taxable event　課税対象となる事象

taxable period　課税対象期間

taxable person　納税義務者

taxable profit　課税所得

taxable purchase　課税仕入れ

taxable value　課税価格

taxable year　課税対象年度

taxation　課税

taxation by estimate　推計課税

taxation on expense of contribution or donation　寄附金課税

taxes and other public charges　租税公課

tax-exempt　非課税の

taxing right　課税権

taxpayer identification number　納税者番号

technical service provision　技術役務の提供

telegraphic transfer buying rate (TTB)　電信買相場

telegraphic transfer middle rate (TTM)　電信相場の中値

telegraphic transfer selling rate (TTS)　電信売相場

temporary payments　仮払金

temporary receipts　仮受金

temporary resident　一時居住者

tenancy agreement　賃貸借契約書

tenancy by the entirety　夫婦での不動産共有

tenancy in common　共有不動産占有権

tentative validity　公定力

term　期限

territorial tax　国外所得免除方式

territorial tax(ation) system　国外所得免除方式

territorial taxation principle　属地主義

testate　生前に有効な遺言書を作成した(人)
例 die testate　遺言を残して死ぬ

testation　遺言による財産処分、遺贈

testator　遺言者

tested company　検証対象法人

theft　盗難

thin capitalisation　過少資本

thin capitalisation rules　過少資本税制

third party　第三者

threshold　閾値、基準値

tie(-)breaker rule　居住地振り分けルール

timber income　山林所得

TIN → taxpayer identification number

title 所有権

TNMM → transactional net margin method

TNMM with full cost mark up as profit indicator 総費用営業利益率を利益指標とするTNMM

TNMM with operating margin as profit indicator 売上高営業利益率を指標とするTNMM

Tokumei Kumiai (TK) 匿名組合

Tokutei Mokuteki Kaisha (TMK) 特定目的会社

tools 工具

TP → transfer pricing

TPM → transfer pricing methodology

trademark right 商標権

transactional net margin method 取引単位営業利益法

transfer 譲渡、譲渡する

transfer cost 譲渡費用

transfer of endorsed note 裏書譲渡

transfer price 移転価格

transfer pricing (TP) 移転価格

transfer pricing adjustment 移転価格調整

transfer pricing document 移転価格文書

transfer pricing documentation 移転価格文書化、移転価格ドキュメンテーション

transfer pricing methodology (TPM) 独立企業間価格算定手法

transfer pricing study 移転価格の検証

transfer pricing taxation 移転価格課税

transfer pricing taxation system 移転価格税制

transfer registration 移転登記

transferee 譲受人

transferee corporation 合併法人

transferor 譲渡人

transferor corporation 被合併法人

transitional measure 経過措置

transitional provision 経過措置規定

translate 為替の換算をする

translation 為替換算

translation difference 為替換算差額

transportation cost 運送費

treasury share [stock] 自己株式

treaty override トリーティオーバーライド（和英見出し参照）

treaty shopping トリーティショッピング（和英見出し参照）、条約漁り

trial 裁判

tribunal 審判所、裁判所

trust 信託

trust deed 信託証書

trust estate 信託財産

trustee 受託者（信託における）

TTB → telegraphic transfer buying rate

TTM → telegraphic transfer middle rate

TTS → telegraphic transfer selling rate

turnover ratio 回転率

two-step approach 二段階アプローチ（恒久的施設帰属所得の算定方法）

U

ultimate parent company 究極の親会社

UN → United Nations

uncontrolled 第三者間の

uncontrolled transaction 第三者間取引

undepreciated balance 未償却残高

under-depreciation amount 減価償却不足額

U
V
W

underpayment 納付過少

underreport 過少申告

undertaxed payments rule (UTPR) 過少課税支払否認ルール

undivided bequest 未分割遺産

unilateral advance pricing arrangement ユニ（ラテラル）APA（和英見出し参照）

unilateral relief 国内法による二重課税の軽減制度

unit trust ユニット・トラスト（和英見出し参照）

United Nations (UN) 国際連盟（国連）

United Nations Model Double Taxation Convention between Developed and Developing Countries 国連モデル租税条約

unlisted stock 非上場株式

unrealised (capital) gain 含み益

unrecorded asset 簿外資産

unrecorded liability 簿外負債

unrelated corporation 非関連者

unrelated party 非関連者

unrelated person 非関連者

usufruct 用益権、使用収益の権利

utility model patent 実用新案権

UTPR → undertaxed payments rule

V

valuation method 評価方法

valuation of assets 資産の評価

valuation of over-the-counter stock 気配相場のある株式の評価

value added tax (VAT) 付加価値税

VAT → value added tax

voluntary adjustment 自己否認

voluntary conveyance 無償譲渡

voluntary depreciation 任意償却

voting right 議決権

W

waiving of inheritance 相続放棄

welfare facility 福利厚生施設

welfare pension 厚生年金

widow 寡婦

widower 寡夫

will 遺言

winding up 清算

window dressing 粉飾決算

with tax 税込み（で、の）

withholding agent 源泉徴収義務者

withholding income tax 源泉所得税

withholding obligation 源泉徴収義務

withholding record 源泉徴収票

withholding tax 源泉税

withholding tax amount table 源泉徴収税額表

without tax 税抜き（で、の）

working student 勤労学生

worksheet 精算表

worldwide income 全世界所得

worldwide system 全世界所得課税方式

write down 帳簿価額の一部評価減

write off 帳簿価額の全額評価減

Y

YK → Yugen Kaisha

Yugen Kaisha (YK) 有限会社

【編者・執筆者紹介】

税理士法人フェアコンサルティング

移転価格コンサルティング、外国子会社合算税制コンサルティング、国際的組織再編コンサルティングなど国際税務分野のコンサルティング、法人税調査や事前確認審査をはじめとする国税当局対応を強みとし、「公正」で「高度」な国際税務ソリューションを提供している。
東京、大阪、シンガポールの直営拠点の他、フェアコンサルティンググループとして世界17か国に30拠点を展開している。

（執筆者）

細田明　税理士

国税庁では国際税務の企画立案、外国税務当局との情報交換、各国税制調査、シンガポール駐在等を担当し、国税局、税務署では大規模法人、外国法人、個人等の税務調査にも従事。

大企業から中小企業に至るまでの幅広い顧客層に対する国際税務コンサルティングを強みとしながら、顧客の海外事業戦略、資本政策、組織再編、国境を超える事業承継、M&Aや資本提携などに関する税務アドバイザリー業務について豊富な経験と実績を有する。また日本・海外税務当局をはじめとする各方面の政府関係者との良好な関係を築きながら海外投資環境の改善にも尽力している。

清水達也　税理士

税務署において、広範囲の税目（酒税・印紙税・法人税・消費税・源泉所得税等）を担当し、各種業種・規模の法人調査、相談等の業務に従事。現在は、豊富な税務知識と経験を基に、国際源泉、恒久的施設（PE）課税、外国子会社合算税制、海外の税制、移転価格文書化業務など、幅広い国際税務のアドバイザリー業務をクライアントに提供している。

長田健嗣　税理士

一般事業会社の経理部で連結決算、税務申告及び上場準備業務等を担当。その後会計事務所にて外資系企業の決算、申告業務及び個人確定申告業務等を行う。税理士法人フェアコンサルティングにおいては、国際源泉課税、外国子会社合算税制及び移転価格税制等の国際税務を中心とした税務相談、コンサルティング業務を提供した。

現在は、税理士法人JCタックスにおいて、主として外資系企業に対し、国内・国際税務に関する税務相談、コンサルティング業務に従事している。

著者との契約により検印省略

令和４年12月30日　初版発行

外国人対応に役立つ
和英対照税務ハンドブック
税制解説の英訳＆税務用語辞典

編　　者　税理士法人
　　　　　フェアコンサルティング
発 行 者　大　坪　克　行
印 刷 所　美研プリンティング株式会社
製 本 所　牧製本印刷株式会社

発行所　〒161-0033　東京都新宿区
下落合２丁目５番13号
株式会社　**税務経理協会**
振替　00190-2-187408
電話 (03) 3953-3301 (編集部)
FAX (03) 3565-3391
(03) 3953-3325 (営業部)
URL　http://www.zeikei.co.jp/
乱丁・落丁の場合は，お取替えいたします。

ISBN978-4-419-06888-2　C3034